UpRooted

By God's Design

30 DAY BIBLE STUDY DEVOTIONAL
ROOTED IN
EZRA 1-6, HAGGAI, AND ZECHARIAH 1

By Jan C. Thompson

AUTHOR OF

Rooted

Woman of Valor

Copyright Notice

Unless otherwise indicated, all Scripture quotations are from the Holy Bible, New International Version* NIV* Copyright ©1973, 1978, 1984, 2011 by Biblica.Inc.* Used by permission. All rights reserved worldwide.

The web addresses referenced in this book were live and correct at the time of the book's publication but may be subject to change.

Cover and interior design: Derick Gentry Thompson
Cover art: Gloria Seitz

Published by Amazon Kindle Direct Publishing
Printed in the United States of America

Email: jancthompson@gmail.com
Website/blog: http://jancthompson.com

Library of Congress Cataloging-in-Publication Data

Thompson, Jan C.
UpRooted by God's Design
30 Day Bible Study Devotional
Rooted in Ezra 1-6, Haggai, and Zechariah 1

ISBN # 979-8-8529-9095-2

Acknowledgments

As I ventured onto this journey to curate a second book from my spiritual life retreats, I paused more often than with my first book, *Rooted Woman of Valor*. Now the finish line for *UpRooted by God's Design* 30 Day Bible Study Devotional is in view.

Once again, my family joined my book team as skilled writers, designers, editors, and prayerful cheerleaders. I cherish each of them! From my daughter, Tiffany, soulful lyrics and music weave their way throughout this uprooted journey to provide creative meditation. My son, Derick, used his digital brilliance to design the front and back covers and launch my book onto Amazon Kindle Direct Publishing.

My brother-in-law, Dr. Gary Gromacki, provided editing. My husband, Rick, and I appreciate his well-honed editing skills and extensive grasp of God's Word as a professor of doctoral students at Calvary University in Kansas City, Missouri.

My ministry friend, Gloria Seitz, painted the watercolor scene on the book cover. As a woman of valor, she offered her generous gift of art to enrich my words. Thank you, Gloria, for ministering with me on a book venture again! You are so talented!

This quote from Mother Teresa reminds me of the unique gifts given by our Lord and Savior for His glory.

"You can do what I cannot do.

I can do what you cannot do.

But together, we can do great things!"

I am grateful for the gracious and godly women who shared my teachings in Mongolia, Germany, the Czech Republic, Hungary, Russia, and the United States. They reflect the deep desire God stirs within His people to know the whole counsel of the Word of God and the deep joy and light it brings to one's soul. I pray this book roots and encourages them and others on their spiritual journeys.

Gratefully,

Jan C. Thompson

Dedication

To my cloud of witnesses,
who encouraged my love of Scripture and taught me
to search for them like one mining for the greatest of treasures

Dr. D.B. Eastep and Dr. Warren Wiersbe
Calvary Baptist Church in Latonia, KY
my childhood pastors, who taught their congregations
to love and search the Scriptures

Mrs. Eastep
Pastor's wife and Christian bookstore manager,
who nurtured my love for studying the Scriptures
by giving me commentaries and other resources
throughout the years

Dr. Mary LeBar and Dr. Lois LeBar
Wheaton College Christian Education professors/sisters,
who taught me the course, Inductive Bible Study Method,
that empowered me to search the Scriptures for myself

John and Ruth Purvis
Wheaton College Navigator leaders,
who provided the vision
and practice of inductive Bible study

Rick Thompson
My husband and ministry partner
to study and teach the Scriptures

David, Derick, and Tiffany
Our children, who graciously let us teach the Scriptures
to them during their childhood and bless us with
the many gifts given to them by their Heavenly Father

Contents

Introduction to *UpRooted by God's Design*   7
Daily, Doable, Deep Devotional—3D Plan   8
Setting the Stage for our UpRooted Journey   10

Introduction to Weeks 1-3   11
Guideposts for Our UpRooted Journey

Week 1   Guideposts for Our Past UpRooted Journey   13
             II Chronicles 36
Week 2   Guideposts for Our Present UpRooted Journey   27
             Ezra 1-2
Week 3   Guideposts for Our Future UpRooted Journey   41
             Ezra 3-4

Introduction to Weeks 4-6   57
God's Rooting Review for Our UpRooted Journey

Week 4   God's 1st Rooting Review—God's Time   59
             Haggai 1
Week 5   God's 2nd Rooting Review—God's Plan   73
             Haggai 2:1-9
        God's 3rd Rooting Review—God's Call   78
             Zechariah 1:1-6
        God's 4th Rooting Review—God's Word (Part 1)   82
             Haggai 2:10-19
Week 6   God's 4th Rooting Review—God's Word (Part 2)   87
             Haggai 2:20-23
        God's Rooting Reviews Applied   Ezra 5-6   90

Conclusion ReRooting by God's Design   103

Toolbox for *UpRooted by God's Design*   105
Daily, Doable, Deep Devotional—3D Plan Template   106
Prayers of JOY (Jesus, Others, You) Template   107
God's Rooting Review for Personal Reflection Template   108
Timeline Chart for Ezra, Haggai, and Zechariah 1   110
Chronological Bible Text of Ezra, Haggai, and Zechariah 1   111
Psalms of the Exiles—Psalms 74, 85, 126, 138, and 139:1-12   124
Full Notes of God's Rooting Review from Haggai and   128
             Zechariah 1
UpRooted by God's Design Book Song Playlist   136
             by Tiffany Thompson
Notes   *UpRooted by God's Design* Resources   137

Introduction
to
UpRooted by God's Design

Uprooted evokes an image of a large tree with its roots dangling out of the ground like a beached octopus longing for the hope of nourishment and a future. Any compassionate gardener wants to rescue its dire situation by finding a way to root it again in its present soil or quickly transplant it. Alongside the plant world, humanity knows the challenges of the uprooted life and journey. During war and famine, uprooting is a matter of survival. The uprooted journey often moves toward the next stage of life, from college, career, new home, marriage, parenting, and retirement.

The idea of being uprooted rarely occurred to me as a young girl. We lived in the house my uncle built until I started high school. The first uprooting I experienced was a strategic move my parents planned to build our new home close to our schools. I enjoyed the short walks for times of reflection. I often sensed God stirring up my spirit to prepare for a lifetime of uprooted journeys.

Decades later, journals of uprooted challenges, struggles, and joys fill my bookshelves. During one uprooted journey, I traveled between Chicago and my high school home in northern Kentucky to support my aging parents. Their naps provided ample Bible study time. I didn't realize how life-changing an inductive study of Ezra 1-6, Haggai, and Zechariah 1:1-6 would become. As you journey with me through this *Uprooted by God's Design* 30 Day Bible Study Devotional, I pray Romans 15:4-7 will be fulfilled in your life, leading to endurance, encouragement, and hope.

Romans 15:4-7 ESV
"For whatever was written in former days was written for our instruction, that through endurance and through the encouragement of the Scriptures we might have hope. May the God of endurance and encouragement grant you to live in such harmony with one another, in accord with Christ Jesus, that together you may with one voice glorify the God and Father of our Lord Jesus Christ. Therefore welcome one another as Christ has welcomed you, for the glory of God."

I welcome you to this study that captures the history and prophecy of one of the uprooted journeys of God's people. I pray the daily, doable, and deep format described on the next page will offer a clear pathway for you to grow on your spiritual journey and to find Biblical insights applicable to your life.

Daily, Doable, Deep Devotional—3D Plan

As you embark on this devotional journey, I desire to provide a 3D experience. The **Daily** reading provides chewable bites of Scripture that will feed your soul like Jeremiah 15:16 expresses, "When your words came, I ate them; they were my joy and heart's delight, for I bear your name, Lord God Almighty."

I've organized the length and timing of the thirty devotionals to be **Doable.** There are five a week for six weeks. That provides time to focus on church and rest on the weekend. The **Deep** insights for your soul will come as you daily journey through the **PRAY** pattern of spiritual disciplines for balanced spiritual growth.

Praise, **R**ead/**R**eflect on His Word, **A**sk in Prayer, and **Y**ield to apply His Word.

Praise—Psalm 71:14
"As for me, I will always have hope; I will praise you more and more."
First, we focus on Scripture that will direct us toward the Lord and praise.

Read/**R**eflect—Psalm 119:105, 18
"Your word is a lamp to my feet, and a light on my path."
"Open my eyes that I might see wonderful things in your law."
Next, we will flow through our focused Scriptures, background, insights into the passage, and space for your reflective journaling. The goal is information that leads to transformation.

Ask—Matthew 7:7
"Ask and it will be given to you; seek and you will find; knock and the door will be open to you."
Take time to jot down and ask the Lord for His Word to work in your heart and others. At the end of each week, there is a Prayers of **JOY** (**J**esus, **O**thers, **Y**ou) page to use for your prayer requests. D.L. Moody said, "Every work of God can be traced to some kneeling form."

Yield—Romans 12:1-2
"Therefore, I urge you, brothers and sisters, in view of God's mercy, to offer your bodies as a living sacrifice, holy and pleasing to God—this is your true and proper worship."
Yield to His teaching, will, and direction by saying. 'Yes,' to the call of the Holy Spirit each day.

When you open God's Word, expect to meet with Him and learn something from Him. We come to our relationship with the Lord with different personalities and ways of learning. In her book *Switch on Your Brain*, Dr. Caroline Leaf reminds us that the best learning occurs with the variety of senses God gave us. The PRAY pattern offers one's voice in praise and prayer, eyes for reading, the mind for reflecting, soul/conscience for yielding, and hands for journaling. At the end of each week, there are Reflective Questions and the Prayers of **JOY** (**J**esus, **O**thers, **Y**ou) page. They are great to use as an individual or with a small group.

I teach this material as a spiritual journey retreat with reflective music sung by my daughter, Tiffany Thompson, a professional singer/songwriter. Her lyrics are woven into various devotional days to provide poetic meditation. We created an online playlist so you can listen to her soul-filled songs as they arrive on this UpRooted Journey. Be sure to find the link on my website listed below. On page 136, there is a list of the songs and their location throughout the book.

Playlist title*:*
UpRooted by God's Design **Book Song Playlist**

Locations to link to the playlist and listen to Tiffany's songs:

- Jan Thompson's website: **jancthompson.com**

- Jan's Link Tree account: **https://linktr.ee/jancthompson**
for quick access to the playlist on Spotify, iTunes, Amazon Music, and SoundCloud music-streaming services.

Setting the Stage for Our UpRooted Journey

In the beginning, God placed His precious creation of man and woman in a beautiful garden to live and grow. But the Garden of Eden had challenges, and Adam and Eve listened to the God-forsaken serpent instead of their Creator. The result was a journey out of Eden into a world of unknowns, hard work, and a marred relationship with their Creator.

Now, that is a journey we wish they had not taken, but sadly, they did! Though His creation disobeyed Him, the Lord of the Universe and His eternal love designed a plan. By uprooting Adam and Eve from the Garden of Eden, God prepared them for the journey back into a spiritual relationship with Him. They turned their eyes and hearts toward their Creator.

From that time on, when God chose to redirect His people, He often designed an uprooted journey. Some examples are:

- Noah was uprooted onto a sea journey when the rest of humanity turned from the living God.
- Abraham, by faith, listened to God's uprooted plan to leave his homeland and journey to the Promised Land.
- Joseph, uprooted from home by the envy of his brothers, became a leader in Egypt by God's design.
- After 400 years under Egyptian control, God chose Moses to uproot and lead His people back to the Promised Land, but disobedience led them into the wilderness for a side journey.

During the 40 years of their wilderness journey, God led the nation of Israel with a cloud by day and fire by night. He guided them to build the mobile tabernacle where His glory dwelt and led them into the Promised Land. God told them to rid the land of destructive enemies on their arrival. God taught His people to listen and live for Him through their judges and kings. Sometimes, they obeyed, but countless times, they did not.

The united kingdom of Israel lasted 120 years under their first three kings, Saul, David, and Solomon. Solomon built the magnificent Temple, where God's glory dwelt. After his death, the kingdom was divided into Israel, the northern kingdom, and Judah, the southern kingdom. In the books of First and Second Kings and Chronicles, we learn that throughout the next 250 years, all the nineteen kings of Israel were evil, and only a few of Judah's kings obeyed the Lord. The Lord sent many prophets to speak for Him. Israel heard clear directions from Elijah, Amos, and Hosea. Judah heard from great prophets, such as Isaiah and Jeremiah. Yet, despite constant warnings by God's prophets, the kings and people of both kingdoms continued in disobedience.

Introduction to Weeks 1-3
Guideposts for Our UpRooted Journey

As we journey into the first three weeks of this devotional, we begin in II Chronicles 36. God pronounces His design of the UpRooted journey after 700 years of rooted Jewish life in the Promised Land. God gave the Old Testament prophet Jeremiah the discouraging but critical role to warn Judah to obey Him before it was too late. When the prophecy of uprooting God's people became the exile from their beloved Promised Land to a land far away, Jeremiah wisely encourages them in Jeremiah 31:21,

"Set up road signs; put up guideposts.
Take note of the highway, the road that you take.
Return, Virgin Israel, return to your towns."

For the first three weeks of the *UpRooted by God's Design* devotional days, look for the guideposts that God provides along this UpRooted Journey's past, present, and future.

The 3D Devotional Plan will be the daily pattern of Praise, Read, Reflect, Ask, and Yield. Prayers of JOY (Jesus, Others, You) page is at the end of each week after the Review—Reflection Questions.

Praise Psalms 74, 85, and 126 will be the praise focus for Weeks 1-3.
Psalm 74 expresses the lament of the exiles heading to Babylon.
Psalms 85 and 126 express praise and gratitude of the returning exiles.

Read

Week	*Theme*	*Timing* 605-520 BC	*Scriptures*	*Page*
Week 1	Guideposts for Our Past UpRooted Journey		II Chronicles 36	13
Week 2	Guideposts for Our Present UpRooted Journey		Ezra 1-2	27
Week 3	Guideposts for Our Future UpRooted Journey		Ezra 3-5	41

Watch for Guideposts along the Uprooted Journey!

There is a time for everything

and a season

for every activity

under the heavens:

a time to be born

and a time to die,

a time to plant

and a time to

UpRoot.

Ecclesiastes 3:1-2

Week 1   Guideposts for Our Past UpRooted Journey

The fulfillment of many prophecies concerning this UpRooted Journey begins with God's pronouncement there is "no remedy" in II Chronicles 36:15-16. Along with that passage, we will reflect on several exilic psalms. Then, we will seek to discover the directions given by the prophet Jeremiah to the exiles. As Jeremiah 31:21 declares, "Set up road signs, put up guideposts. Take note of the highway, the road that you take." We will look for specific guideposts that the Scriptures provide for the Jewish exiles and reflect on their insights for our spiritual journey.

Praise   Psalm 74 expresses the exiles' sorrow on their way to Babylon.

Rooting Idea   After journeying through Day 1-5 devotionals, take the time to review the reflective questions at the end of the week. They are good to use for a small group study. Progressively, fill-in the Prayer Page of JOY (Jesus, Others, You) located after the Review page.

Read

Day	Theme	Timing	Scriptures	Page
		605-586 BC		
Day 1	Guidepost 1—Root of the UpRooted Journey			14
			II Chronicles 36:15-16	
Day 2	Guidepost 2—Psalm of the UpRooted to Babylon			16
			Psalm 74:1-12	
Day 3	Guidepost 3—Psalm of the UpRooted in Babylon			18
			Psalm 137	
Day 4	Guidepost 4—Hope on the UpRooted Journey			20
			Jeremiah 27:21-22	
Day 5	Guidepost 5—Instructions on the UpRooted Journey			22
			Jeremiah 29:1-14	
Week 1	Review—Reflective Questions for Individual and Small Group			24

Look for God's Guidepost for you each day!

Day 1   Guidepost 1—Root of the UpRooted Journey

II Chronicles 36:15-16
Timing—605 BC

Praise   Psalm 74:12
"But God is my King from long ago; he brings salvation on the earth."

Read

In 722 B.C., the Assyrian kingdom conquered the ten northern tribes of Israel as God's prophets warned. Judah, the southern kingdom consisting of two tribes, continued for 100 years because of the obedience of a few of their kings. However, disobedience started to permeate the culture again. God warns Judah about His coming judgment in this chilling, final chapter of their pre-exilic history.

II Chronicles 36:15-16 states,
"The LORD, the God of their ancestors, sent word to them through his messengers again and again, because he had pity on his people and on his dwelling place, (His Temple in Jerusalem). But they mocked God's messengers, despised his words, and scoffed at his prophets until the wrath of the LORD was aroused against his people and there was no remedy."

Reflect

- What was the root problem of God's people that brought this "no remedy" time?

- What do we learn about the heart and ways of God?

- When has the Lord sent His Word to you? How did you listen?

Ask the Lord for ears that hear and a heart to obey as you pray for yourself and others.

Yield to the wisdom and promptings the Lord gives you each day.

Your UpRooted Journal to Reflect, Ask, and Yield
Throughout the devotional, this journal space will allow you to write more of your thoughts from the Reflect, Ask, and Yield ideas. The area will vary based on the day.

Guidepost 1—Look for the root of the UpRooted journey.

Day 2   Guidepost 2—Psalm of the UpRooted to Babylon   Psalm 74:1-12
Timing—605-586 BC

Praise   Psalm 74:13a, 15a
"It was you who split open the seas by your power.
It was you who opened up springs and streams."

Read
From 605-586 BC, the "no remedy" judgment came to God's people. King Nebuchadnezzar of the Babylonian Empire captured the Jews in three stages. The final surge was in 586 BC. With his mighty armies, they ruthlessly destroyed the beautiful capital of Jerusalem and the magnificent Temple that Solomon built. In the last chapter of pre-exilic history, II Chronicles 36:20-21 says, "He carried into exile to Babylon the remnant, who escaped from the sword, and they became servants to him and his successors until the kingdom of Persia came to power. The land enjoyed its sabbath rests; all the time of its desolation it rested, until the seventy years were completed in fulfillment of the word of the LORD spoken by Jeremiah." (Refers to Jeremiah 25:11)

This UpRooted Journey out of the Promised Land came almost 700 years after Moses died, and Joshua conquered Jericho to lead them into the Promised Land. There were always singers and songwriters among the Jewish people, even on their coerced UpRooted Journey to Babylon. Specific Psalms captured God's people's hearts, questions, and faith as they marched along the arduous trek. We will reflect on several of them this week.

Psalm 74
1 "O God, why have you rejected us forever?
   Why does your anger smolder against the sheep of your pasture?
2 Remember the nation you purchased long ago, the people of your inheritance,
   whom you redeemed—Mount Zion, where you dwelt.
3 Turn your steps toward these everlasting ruins,
   all this destruction the enemy has brought on the sanctuary.
4 Your foes roared in the place where you met with us;
   they set up their standards as signs.
5 They behaved like men wielding axes
   to cut through a thicket of trees.
6 They smashed all the carved paneling with their axes and hatchets.
7 They burned your sanctuary to the ground;
   they defiled the dwelling place of your Name.
8 They said in their hearts, "We will crush them completely!"
   They burned every place where God was worshiped in the land.
9 We are given no signs from God;
   no prophets are left, and none of us knows how long this will be.
10 How long will the enemy mock you, God?
   Will the foe revile your name forever?

16

11 Why do you hold back your hand, your right hand?
   Take it from the folds of your garment and destroy them!
12 But God is my King from long ago; he brings salvation on the earth."

Reflect
- What are the exiles' attitudes toward God?

- What are the prayers of their hearts?

- Where are they finding hope?

Ask the Lord to guide you to His answers and promises of hope for you and others.

Yield to the wisdom the Lord provides for your UpRooted journeys.

Your UpRooted Journal to Reflect, Ask, and Yield
Listen/read Tiffany Thompson's lyrics that express the heartache of this exiled journey. (*UpRooted by God's Design* Book Song Playlist on jancthompson.com)

"Smoke and Fire" by Tiffany Thompson and Rye Richmond
We used to be kings and queens, young and bold
Bringing to life our imaginings with hopes of gold
There was a time when we would lift each other up to touch the sky
Knitting the stars one by one as they passed by

Now, we're walking through fire, smoke, and fire
With every footstep, the flames get higher
Everything that we thought we knew is disappearing in a golden hue
It's fire, smoke, and fire; we're walking through fire, smoke, and fire

I can recall the day it all changed
The safe place we held dear was torn away
We left our home in the middle of the night with just our lives
Every dream, every hope instilled, got left behind

Fire and smoke, every footstep takes me closer to a higher power

---

Guidepost 2—Sing psalms of lament on the UpRooted journey.

Day 3   Guidepost 3—Psalm of the Uprooted in Babylon   Psalm 137
Timing—605-586 BC

Praise   Psalm 74:16
"The day is yours, and yours also is the night;
you established the sun and moon."

Read
As God's UpRooted people arrived near Babylon, their hearts were heavy as they
longed for the past and feared the future. As you read Psalm 137, reflect on what
they experienced and learned during these difficult days.

Psalm 137
"By the rivers of Babylon, we sat down and wept,
when we remembered Zion.
2 There on the poplars, we hung our harps
3 for there our captors asked us for songs;
our tormentors demanded songs of joy;
They said, "Sing us one of the songs of Zion!"
4 How can we sing the songs of the LORD while in a foreign land?
5 If I forget you, Jerusalem, may my right hand forget its skill.
6 May my tongue cling to the roof of my mouth if I do not remember you,
if I do not consider Jerusalem, my highest joy.
7 Remember, LORD, what the Edomites did on the day Jerusalem fell.
"Tear it down" they cried, "tear it down to its foundations!"
8 Daughter Babylon, doomed to destruction
happy is the one who repays you according to what you have done to us.
9 Happy is the one who seizes your infants and
dashes them against the rocks."

Reflect
- What are the exiles' specific struggles and attitudes toward their captors?

- Where do they focus their hope?

- What brings perspective during your challenging or uprooted times?

Ask the Lord to strengthen you and others in difficult times of life.

Yield to the insights the Lord provides for your challenging days.

Your UpRooted Journal to Reflect, Ask, and Yield
Try to write a psalm about a difficult time on your journey.
Be honest and open as you pour your heart out to the Lord.

Guidepost 3—Remember God's goodness on the UpRooted journey.

Day 4 Guidepost 4—Hope on the UpRooted Journey Jeremiah 27:21-22

Timing—605-586 BC

Praise Psalm 74:17
"It was you who set all the boundaries of the earth;
you made both summer and winter."

Read
On the journey to Babylon, joy had bottomed out for the Jewish exiles. They were heartbroken and confused, though they knew they were blessed to be alive. In Psalm 74 and 137, we hear their heart cry. Was there anything past the end of their nation and lives? What did their future look like?

The Lord provides a future and hope past this end of their history, though it will not make sense to His people for a long time. Along with the captives, Nebuchadnezzar and his armies confiscate precious items from Solomon's Temple. A glimmer of hope is offered in Jeremiah 27:21-22.

"Yes, this is what the LORD Almighty, the God of Israel, says about the things that are left in the house of the LORD and in the palace of the king of Judah and in Jerusalem: 'They will be taken to Babylon and there they will remain until the day I come for them,' declares the LORD. Then, I will bring them back and restore them to this place."

Reflect
- How does Jeremiah 27:21-22 provide a glimmer of hope for the exiled Jews?

Ask the Lord to help you and others process through uprooted days of uncertainty.

Yield to the work of God in your past and present.

Your UpRooted Journal to Reflect, Ask, and Yield
Read/listen to Tiffany's lyrics, "Past This End," as a prayer to the Lord, and reflect on a time when you felt distant from Him and needed hope. Journal your prayer.

"Past This End" by Tiffany Thompson
I didn't know that it would go down this way, all forms fading into gray
I recall leaning on Your chest, my heels locked to Your path
Our pulses synced, my beat Your Own
When You said that You would love me always, did You mean past this end?
My mind knows our life is over, and this is something we can't mend

One million 'I love yous' quickly fade out of view
Silent fights take their place; Your feet are far from my own
Your pulse is gone; I'm alone
When You said that You would love me always, did You mean past this end?
My mind knows our life is over, and this is something we can't mend
Maybe love lives past this end

Guidepost 4—Look for hope on the UpRooted Journey.

Day 5 Guidepost 5—Instructions of Hope on the Uprooted Journey

Jeremiah 29:1-14
Timing—605-586 BC

Praise Psalm 74:21
"Do not let the oppressed retreat in disgrace;
may the poor and needy praise your name."

Read
As the exiles arrived in Babylon, God prompted the prophet Jeremiah, who was still in Jerusalem, to write them a letter with instructions on how to live in the land of their captivity. He provided answers to their questions with words of hope.

Jeremiah 29:1-14
"This is the text of the letter that the prophet Jeremiah sent from Jerusalem to the surviving elders among the exiles and to the priests, the prophets and all the other people Nebuchadnezzar had carried into exile from Jerusalem to Babylon."
(Verses 2-3 record the timing and who delivered the letter.)

4 "It said:
This is what the LORD Almighty, the God of Israel, says to all those I carried into exile from Jerusalem to Babylon:

5 "Build houses and settle down; plant gardens and eat what they produce.
6 Marry and have sons and daughters; find wives for your sons and give your daughters in marriage, so that they too may have sons and daughters. Increase in number there; do not decrease. 7 Also, seek the peace and prosperity of the city to which I have carried you into exile. Pray to the LORD for it, because if it prospers, you too will prosper."

8 Yes, this is what the LORD Almighty, the God of Israel, says: "Do not let the prophets and diviners among you deceive you. Do not listen to the dreams you encourage them to have. 9 They are prophesying lies to you in My name. I have not sent them," declares the LORD.

10 This is what the LORD says:
"When seventy years are completed for Babylon, I will come to you and fulfill my good promise to bring you back to this place. 11 For I know the plans I have for you," declares the LORD, "plans to prosper you and not to harm you, plans to give you hope and a future. 12 Then you will call on me and come and pray to me, and I will listen to you. 13 You will seek me and find me when you seek me with all your heart. 14 I will be found by you," declares the LORD, "and will bring you back from captivity. I will gather you from all the nations and places where I have banished you," declares the LORD, "and will bring you back to the place from which I carried you into exile."

Reflect
- What directions did the Lord give His people on how to become rooted in Babylon?

- What specifics about their future and hope did He provide?

Ask the Lord to help you recognize His guideposts for your spiritual journey.

Yield to the Lord's wisdom on how to live where He plants you.

Your UpRooted Journal to Reflect, Ask, and Yield
Read/listen to Tiffany's song, "New Communions," and reflect on a time when you were in a new and challenging situation with adjustments to rebuild your home and relationships.

"New Communions" by Tiffany Thompson and Luke Brindley
Welcome new communions
Let go of your pain and burdens
Admission is free, just confess you're a human
With a heart open wide to new communions

The darkness of night doesn't stand a chance
With fire and starlight starting to dance
On the faces of friends, all gathered round
The life in this moment, what's lost is found

Building a home and breaking some bread
Making the time to really listen
You are a mystery I want to explore
A distant horizon as close as the shore

Storms rage around us
But love has found us
Right where we are

Guidepost 5—Listen for instructions of hope on the UpRooted journey.

Week 1 Review
Reflective Questions for Individual and Small Group

1. **Praise** What praise verse was your favorite this week? Why?

2. **Read** What Scriptural insight challenged you the most this week?

3. **Reflect** What were some of your reflections in your UpRooted Journal?

4. **Ask** What are you asking the Lord to do in your life and others this week?

5. **Yield** How is the Lord working in your life to yield to His promptings?

6. What **guidepost** are you making and taking with you this week?

Prayers of JOY
(Jesus, Others, You)

Jesus, I'm thankful for

Others' Prayer Needs

Your Prayer Needs

This is what the LORD says:

"Stand at the crossroads and look;

Ask for the ancient paths,

Ask where the good way is,

And you will find rest for your souls.

Jeremiah 6:16

Week 2   Guideposts for Our Present UpRooted Journey

For seventy years, the Jewish people increased in number in the world-renowned city of Babylon. God used many of His people, like Daniel, to influence the Babylonian culture and kings. But God promised in Isaiah 44:28, written 200 years before it took place, that He had a plan to use His servant, Cyrus, to provide the opportunity for His exiled people to return to the Promised Land. This week, we will see how God moves in some Jews to go and others to give. Zerubbabel and Joshua are the leaders of those who were uprooted from Babylon. About 50,000 Jewish exiles answered God's call to return and rebuild the Temple in Jerusalem.

Praise   Psalm 85 is a prayer of repentance as the exiles return to Jerusalem.

Rooting Idea   After journeying through Day 6-10 devotionals, take the time to review the reflective questions at the end of the week. They are good to use for a small group study. Progressively, fill-in the Prayer Page of JOY (Jesus, Others, You) located after the Review page.

Read

Day	Theme	Timing 536 BC	Scriptures	Page
Day 6	Guidepost 6—God Moves in Us to Provide Direction		Ezra 1:1-4	28
Day 7	Guidepost 7—God Moves in Us toward His Will		Ezra 1:5	30
Day 8	Guidepost 8—God Moves in Us to Provide Resources		Ezra 1:6-11	32
Day 9	Guidepost 9—God Moves in Us toward His Direction		Ezra 2:1-67	34
Day 10	Guidepost 10—God Moves in Us toward His Priorities		Ezra 2:68-70	36
Week 2	Review—Reflective Questions for Individual and Small Group			38

Yield to God's Guideposts that move you toward Him!

Day 6   Guidepost 6—God Moves in Us to Provide Direction   Ezra 1:1-4
Timing—536 BC

Praise   Psalm 85:1-3

"You, LORD, showed favor to your land; you restored the fortunes of Jacob. You forgave the iniquity of your people and covered all their sins. You set aside all your wrath and turned from your fierce anger."

Read   Ezra 1:1-4

"In the first year of Cyrus king of Persia, in order to fulfill the word of the LORD spoken by Jeremiah, the LORD moved the heart of Cyrus king of Persia to make a proclamation throughout his realm and also to put it in writing:

2 "This is what Cyrus king of Persia says:

"'The LORD, the God of heaven, has given me all the kingdoms of the earth and he has appointed me to build a temple for him at Jerusalem in Judah. 3 Any of his people among you may go up to Jerusalem in Judah and build the temple of the LORD, the God of Israel, the God who is in Jerusalem, and may their God be with them. 4 And in any locality where survivors may now be living, the people are to provide them with silver and gold, with goods and livestock, and with freewill offerings for the temple of God in Jerusalem.'"

The call to return to the Promised Land after 70 years arrived! The prophecies were coming true—God's people could return to Jerusalem. The call came from King Cyrus, the very name prophesied 200 years before in Isaiah 44:28, "Who says of Cyrus, 'He is my shepherd and will accomplish all that I please; he will say of Jerusalem, "Let it be rebuilt," and of the temple, "Let its foundations be laid."'"

We see that God sovereignly knows the exact timing and leaders of the exiled Jews. Nothing surprises Him! G. Campbell Morgan states in his book, *The Unfolding Message of the Bible,* "No king was ever born, and no dictator has ever lived who is independent of God."

Reflect

- What specific proclamations did God move in Cyrus' heart for His exiled people?

- What decisions did the exiles need to make?

Ask the Lord to move in your heart to answer His call on your life.

Yield to the movement of the Lord in your heart today. Say Yes!

Your UpRooted Journal to Reflect, Ask, and Yield
- Read/listen to Tiffany's song, "Bed of Decision," as you reflect on the decisions before you today.
- How is God moving in your heart?

"Bed of Decision" by Tiffany Thompson and Luke Brindley
Sooner than later
We'll finally awake
In a bed of decision with the choices we have to face
Sooner than later

Look in a mirror, when did we lose control
Feel the resistance cripples my weary soul

Our lives may lead to eternity
When everything is washed into the sea
Life will bend into shape by the choices we make
Sing a song of right and wrong
Until kingdom comes with the dawn

Over and over, You've given me Your hand
Slowly revealing the grace You release on man

Guidepost 6—God moves in us to provide direction.

Day 7   Guidepost 7—God Moves in Us toward His Will   Ezra 1:5

Timing—536 BC

Praise   Psalm 85:4-5

"Restore us again, God our Savior, and put away your displeasure toward us.
Will you be angry with us forever?
Will you prolong your anger through all generations?"

Read   Ezra 1:5

"Then the family heads of Judah and Benjamin, and the priests and Levites—
everyone whose heart God had moved—prepared to go up and build the house of
the LORD in Jerusalem."

God moved in the heart of King Cyrus to provide the way out of exile and into the
Promised Land. Next, God moved in the hearts of His people. Every family and
person could decide if this was God's call and timing for them. Over the seventy
years of exile, the magnificent city of Babylon became their home. Uprooting
spelled sacrifice. The destination of Judah was now in ruins. But the Lord moved
in those He prepared for this challenging assignment and journey.

Here are five ways to discern God's Will on our spiritual journey.

1.   Word of God (Read and Reflect)
2.   Prayer (Ask)
3.   Holy Spirit's movement in your heart (Yield)
4.   Counsel from godly people (Ask)
5.   Circumstances converge with the first four keys (Watch and Yield)

Reflect
- How are the five key ideas to discerning God's Will taking place in Ezra
  1:1-5?

Ask the Lord to continue to clarify His Word, methods, and movement toward
His will in your life and others on your prayer list.

Yield to the movement of the Lord in your heart and His will for you. Say Yes!

Your UpRooted Journal to Reflect, Ask, and Yield
Journal how the Lord is moving in your life with the key ways to discern His will.
- Verses from Scripture
- Prayers
- Nudging of the Holy Spirit
- Specific counsel from others
- Circumstances that converge with the above input

Guidepost 7—God moves in us toward His will.

Day 8 Guidepost 8—God Moves in Us to Provide Resources Ezra 1:6-11
Timing—536 BC

Praise Psalm 85:6-7
"Will you not revive us again, that your people may rejoice in you?
Show us your unfailing love, LORD, and grant us your salvation."

Read Ezra 1:6-11
"All their neighbors assisted them with articles of silver and gold, with goods and livestock, and with valuable gifts, in addition to all the freewill offerings.
7 Moreover, King Cyrus brought out the articles belonging to the temple of the LORD, which Nebuchadnezzar had carried away from Jerusalem and had placed in the temple of his god.
8 Cyrus king of Persia had them brought by Mithredath the treasurer, who counted them out to Sheshbazzar the prince of Judah.
9 This was the inventory: gold dishes 30, silver dishes 1,000, silver pans 29,
10 gold bowls 30, matching silver bowls 410, other articles 1,000
11 In all, there were 5,400 articles of gold and of silver. Sheshbazzar brought all these along with the exiles when they came up from Babylon to Jerusalem."

In verse 6, God moves in the Jews who will not be going on this Uprooted journey to give generously to those called to go. In Ezra 1:4, King Cyrus presented this challenge, "And in any locality where survivors may now be living, the people are to provide them with silver and gold, with goods and livestock, and with freewill offerings for the temple of God in Jerusalem."

In God's kingdom plan, some are moved to give, and others are moved to go. Our Thompson family found this passage an insightful directive as we prepared to uproot from Iowa and move to Moscow, Russia, as missionaries in 1992. God moved in our hearts to go. Within nine months, He moved in the heart of our church, where we were pastor and wife, to provide the needed ministry support along with thirteen other churches and many individuals. They gave faithfully during the five years of our missionary ministry. It was an incredible, UpRooted journey for our family.

In verses 7-11, God moved in King Cyrus to retrieve and count the 5,400 articles that Babylon confiscated from the Jewish Temple before destroying it. Henrietta Mears notes in *What the Bible is All About*, "God used Babylon as the safety deposit vault for the silver and gold vessels for the Temple." Now, His servant, King Cyrus, returns it all to Jerusalem by way of the exiles for the rebuilding of the Temple.

Reflect
- Journal about a time when you saw the Lord move in others and yourself to do His Will. How and where did He direct you? How did He provide needed resources?

32

Ask the Lord to provide the direction and resources you need for His call on your life today and in the future. Pray the same for those He is moving you to resource through prayer or action.

Yield to the gracious God of the universe and all His good gifts for you!

Your UpRooted Journal to Reflect, Ask, and Yield
Read/listen to Tiffany's song, "In the Distance," to reflect on hearing God's voice to join His journey.

"In the Distance" by Tiffany Thompson and Gyom Amphoux
Western train, I've been waiting here for hours and days now
You called my name, but my baggage and feet don't seem to move on
Should I forget and let go of, stick to dreams in the distance
Western train, is the rumble on the tracks the sound of leaving this place behind?

Whoa, the time is now for you to join me
Oh, this train is heading out to greener valleys
Whoa, the sun is out, come on, let's chase it
Oh, this train is heading out to greener valleys

We've got fears, but come on, let's throw unbelief out the backdoor
Look around, everyone is traveling closer to the future
Oh, you've got to leave, it's time now!

Guidepost 8—God moves in us to provide resources.

Day 9   Guidepost 9—God Moves in Us toward His Direction   Ezra 2:1-67
Timing—536 BC

Praise   Psalm 85:8-9
"I will listen to what God the LORD says; he promises peace to his people,
his faithful servants—but let them not turn to folly. Surely his salvation is near
those who fear him, that his glory may dwell in our land."

Read   Ezra 2:1-2
"Now these are the people of the province who came up from the captivity of the
exiles, whom Nebuchadnezzar king of Babylon had taken captive to Babylon
(they returned to Jerusalem and Judah, each to their own town, in company with
Zerubbabel, Joshua, Nehemiah, Seraiah, Reelaiah, Mordecai, Bilshan, Mispar,
Bigvai, Rehum and Baanah):
The list of the men of the people of Israel:"

Zerubbabel and Joshua were the leaders of this Uprooted Journey. Zerubbabel,
whose name means 'one sown or born in Babylon,' was from the tribe of Judah.
His grandfather, King Jeconiah, was taken captive to Babylon. His father,
Shealtiel, was too old to make the journey. He was joined by Joshua, as the lead
priest, for this first UpRooted Journey of willing exiles. There would be three
waves of returns from the Babylonian exile to the Promised Land.

1.   With Zerubbabel (538-515 BC) Time to rebuild the Temple
     Then, a gap of 57 years
2.   With Ezra (458-456 BC) Time of reformation of the people
     Then, a gap of 12 years
3.   With Nehemiah (444-432 BC) Time for the wall of Jerusalem to be built,
     Nehemiah returned a second time in 430 BC. It would be 400 more years
     before Christ journeyed from heaven to the Promised Land.
     (Note: Timeline Chart is in the Toolbox on page 110.)

Ezra 2:3-63 contains the list of the male head and count of each family group.
There were 33 family groups totaling 23,566, 4363 priests and Levites, 128
musicians, 139 gatekeepers of the temple, 392 temple servants and descendants
of the servants of Solomon, 652 who could not show their family records, as well
as priests who couldn't find their records. (Note: Full biblical text is in the
Toolbox on pages 112-114.)

Ezra 2:64-67 summarizes, "The whole company numbered 42,360, besides their
7,337 male and female slaves; and they also had 200 male and female singers.
They had 736 horses, 245 mules, 435 camels and 6,720 donkeys."

Can you imagine the challenges awaiting this caravan heading west to Jerusalem
with 50,000 people and 8,000 animals, along with the weight and responsibility
of transporting 5,400 articles of gold, silver, gifts, and each family's belongings?

This uprooted journey took about four months as the 50,000 returning exiles walked 900 miles, approximately the distance from Chicago to Orlando, Florida.

Along with the excitement was the challenge to choose to go. Many Jews decided to stay in Babylon, whether it was for the culture, education, relationships, or comfort. They knew the UpRooted destination of Jerusalem was a place of seventy years of decay.

As our family anticipated the UpRooted 5000-mile journey to become missionaries in Russia, we had many decisions and emotions like the exiles. How would the kids transition to a new culture? Would we feel at home? Would we accomplish what God was moving in us to do?

Reflect
Journal about these reflections:
- What is the most life-changing commitment you made to God?
- How did it involve a new adventure?
- What did He teach you in the process? What were your questions?

Ask the Lord to help you follow His movement in your life. If He calls you to lead others, pray for the wisdom and strength to obey.

Yield to the Spirit's movement in your heart today!

Your UpRooted Journal to Reflect, Ask, and Yield

Guidepost 9—God moves in us toward His direction.

Day 10   Guidepost 10—God Moves in Us toward His Priorities

Ezra 2:68-70
Timing—536 BC

Praise   Psalm 85:10-13

"Love and faithfulness meet together; righteousness and peace kiss each other. Faithfulness springs forth from the earth, and righteousness looks down from heaven. The LORD will indeed give what is good, and our land will yield its harvest. Righteousness goes before him and prepares the way for his steps."

Read   Ezra 2:68-70

"When they arrived at the house of the LORD in Jerusalem, some of the heads of the families gave freewill offerings toward the rebuilding of the house of God on its site. 69 According to their ability they gave to the treasury for this work 61,000 darics (1,100 pounds) of gold, 5,000 minas (3 tons) of silver and 100 priestly garments. 70 The priests, the Levites, the musicians, the gatekeepers and the temple servants settled in their own towns, along with some of the other people, and the rest of the Israelites settled in their towns."

God called this group of His people to leave the land of their captivity and return to Jerusalem after 70 years to rebuild His Temple, destroyed by Nebuchadnezzar. The task was overwhelming as they made their way into the devastation of Jerusalem and the Temple area. Still, the heads of the families focused on their priority to honor their God.

Their main priority was to set aside God's part before everything else. So, they stopped near the Temple site to give their freewill offerings toward the rebuilding. They gave freely and generously according to their ability, above and beyond the resources from King Cyrus and the Jews who stayed in Babylon. Their second priority was to settle into their cities, homes, and life after such a monumental move for their families. God knew their best work would be done after their families felt settled and safe.

In 1992, our family of five landed in Moscow, Russia, with ten suitcases and thanked the Lord for a safe UpRooted journey. We knew the first task was to settle in a safe place. It took us about four months to find the apartment, receive our belongings, and figure out where to find food and other supplies. About the same amount of time, it took the returning exiles to settle into their new homes.

Reflect

Journal about a time when you took an uprooted or challenging journey.

- How were you challenged to focus on God's priorities?

- What and who helped you feel settled and rooted again?

Ask the Lord to give you insights into His priorities as you seek Him.

Yield to the wisdom the Lord provides to focus on His priorities for you!

Your UpRooted Journal to Reflect, Ask, and Yield
Read/listen to Tiffany's song, "Home," and focus on your relationship with the Lord being your home even when you feel UpRooted and tired of traveling.

"Home" by Tiffany Thompson and Phil Danyew
I saw you there at the edge
Soles are thin from walking
All alone from far away, eyes are tired from searching

Maybe I'm the end of your road
Maybe I'm the hand you will hold
Throw away those maps, this can be your chance
You do not need to be alone
Look into my eyes, pull me to your side
I will be your home

Sit with me on the ledge, forever more feet dangling
Confide in me every fear, come what may, I'll be here

Everywhere we go, we'll know we'll find a way
Side by side, we are a brighter day
Love so deep, there are no words left to say

Guidepost 10—God moves in us toward His priorities.

Week 2 Review
Reflective Questions for Individual and Small Group

1. **Praise** What praise verse was your favorite this week? Why?

2. **Read** What Scriptural insight challenged you the most this week?

3. **Reflect** What were some of your reflections in your UpRooted Journal?

4. **Ask** What are you asking the Lord to do in your life and others this week?

5. **Yield** How is the Lord working in your life to yield to His promptings?

6. What **guidepost** are you making and taking with you this week?

Prayers of JOY
(Jesus, Others, You)

Jesus, I'm thankful for

Others' Prayer Needs

Your Prayer Needs

Week 3   Guideposts for Our Future UpRooted Journey
Ezra 3-4

After four months of settling into their homes, the priority became to clear the Temple foundation and build the Lord's altar. Ezra 3-4 tells the story of the challenges and joys that God's people experience when they focus on obedience and work as His people for eternal goals and His glory.

Praise Psalm 126 is a Psalm expressing the real joy of the returning exiles.

Rooting Idea After journeying through Day 11-15 devotionals, take the time to review the reflective questions at the end of the week. They are good to use for a small group study. Progressively, fill-in the Prayer Page of JOY (Jesus, Others, You) located after the Review page.

Read

Day	Theme	Timing 537-535 BC	Scriptures	Page
Day 11	Guidepost 11—Focus on Removing Rubble to Rebuild the Altar Ezra 3:1-6			42
Day 12	Guidepost 12—Focus on Working as a Team	Ezra 3:7-9		44
Day 13	Guidepost 13—Focus on Praising God for His Faithfulness Ezra 3:10-13			46
Day 14	Guidepost 14—Focus on Gratitude and Songs of Joy Psalm 126			48
Day 15	Guidepost 15—Focus on Following God, not Fearing Man Ezra 4:1-24			50

Weeks 1-3 Review—Reflective Questions for Individual and Small Group   53

Yield to God's Guidepost—God's focus should be our priority.

Day 11   Guidepost 11—Focus on Removing Rubble to Rebuild the Altar
Ezra 3:1-6
Timing—537 BC, 7th month

Praise   Psalm 126:1
"When the Lord restored the fortunes of Zion, we were like those who dreamed."

Read   Ezra 3:1-6
"When the seventh month came and the Israelites had settled in their towns, the people assembled together as one in Jerusalem. 2 Then Joshua son of Jozadak and his fellow priests and Zerubbabel son of Shealtiel and his associates began to build the altar of the God of Israel to sacrifice burnt offerings on it, in accordance with what is written in the Law of Moses the man of God.
3 Despite their fear of the peoples around them, they built the altar on its foundation and sacrificed burnt offerings on it to the LORD, both the morning and evening sacrifices. 4 Then in accordance with what is written, they celebrated the Festival of Tabernacles with the required number of burnt offerings prescribed for each day. 5 After that, they presented the regular burnt offerings, the New Moon sacrifices and the sacrifices for all the appointed sacred festivals of the LORD, as well as those brought as freewill offerings to the LORD. 6 On the first day of the seventh month they began to offer burnt offerings to the LORD, though the foundation of the LORD's temple had not yet been laid."

Note: The 7th month was the appointed time of three Jewish festivals held around our September-October. The Lord gave these appointed times to Moses in Leviticus 23 and Numbers 29.
1st day—Feast of Trumpets is a Sabbath rest and sacred assembly with trumpet blasts.
10th day—the Day of Atonement, is the most solemn and holy day when the high priest made the annual sacrifice to pay for his and people's sins.
15th-22nd days—Feast of Tabernacles is a week-long celebration to live in booths (temporary shelters of branches) to remember the forty years they lived uprooted in the wilderness under God's care.

The third priority was to set up the altar of the Lord. Before building the Temple, the altar was essential for reestablishing the sacrificial system that set the exiles apart as a nation. They could bring sacrifices, offerings, and celebrations as ordained in the Law. To accomplish this task, they needed to focus on removing enough rubble from the Temple's foundation to make space for the altar, priests, and sacrifices. Verse 3 indicates they built the altar despite fearing the neighboring people's reaction. Fear will come upon us whenever we journey with the Lord toward obedience. Their obedience laid the foundation for the future arrival of Jesus Christ—the final sacrifice—to enter this Temple in 500 years.

Ezra's chapters 2-3 provide the initial three priorities to focus on when uprooted.
1. Set aside what is God's part before anything else.
2. Settle into the basics of life to provide the foundation to become rooted again.
3. Set up your personal altar area to live out Romans 12:1-2 every day before focusing on tyour call and ministries.
Romans 12:1-2 challenges us, "Therefore, I urge you, brothers and sisters, in view of God's mercy, to offer your bodies as a living sacrifice, holy and pleasing to God—this is your true and proper worship. Do not conform to the pattern of this world, but be transformed by the renewing of your mind. Then you will be able to test and approve what God's will is—his good, pleasing and perfect will."

In our new city of ten million people, where we planned to church plant, we knew we needed to find a place of worship for our family, so we had the Lord as our focus before anything else. The Lord led us to the church plant that became the base of our ministry. Decades later, we still minister with that church. Along with settling in during our first months in Moscow, I learned how important it was to remove enough rubble to provide space in our apartment to set up my personal altar time before the Lord.

Reflect
Journal your thoughts.
- What did you learn about God as your Guide from these verses?

- What rubble do you need to remove from your life to have an established personal altar time before the Lord?

Ask the Lord to help you remove the rubble that hinders your time with Him.

Yield to the Lord's call to offer yourself as a living sacrifice, holy and pleasing to Him.

Your UpRooted Journal to Reflect, Ask, and Yield

Guidepost 11—Focus on removing the rubble to rebuild the altar!

Day 12 Guidepost 12—Focus on Working Effectively as a Team

Timing—536 BC, 2nd month

Praise Psalm 126:2

"Our mouths were filled with laughter, our tongues with songs of joy.
Then it was said among the nations, "The LORD has done great things for them.""

Read Ezra 3:7-9

"Then they gave money to the masons and carpenters and gave food and drink
and olive oil to the people of Sidon and Tyre, so that they would bring cedar logs
by sea from Lebanon to Joppa, as authorized by Cyrus king of Persia.
8 In the second month of the second year after their arrival at the house of God in
Jerusalem, Zerubbabel son of Shealtiel, Joshua son of Jozadak and the rest of the
people (the priests and the Levites and all who had returned from the captivity to
Jerusalem) began the work. They appointed Levites twenty years old and older to
supervise the building of the house of the LORD. 9 Joshua and his sons and
brothers and Kadmiel and his sons (descendants of Hodaviah) and the sons of
Henadad and their sons and brothers—all Levites—joined together in supervising
those working on the house of God."

The altar was in use for the first time since the exile. The next monumental task
was building the Temple set forth by the proclamation of King Cyrus. We see the
excellent leadership, planning, delegation, and supervision that Zerubbabel and
Joshua provided to build the needed teams.

Reflect

- What different teams are at work in these verses?

- For another look at God's value of teamwork, read or listen to Exodus
  18 and journal your insights.

- What team are you on at this point? How are you applying team
  principles?

44

Ask the Lord for His wisdom on how to work well with the teams in your life, such as family, work, friends, and others, to accomplish the goals He has set before you.

Yield to God's wisdom about working on a team instead of trying to do things by yourself.

Your UpRooted Journal to Reflect, Ask, and Yield
Journal some thoughts or prayers on your heart today.

Guidepost 12—Focus on working effectively as a team.

Day 13   Guidepost 13—Focus on Praising God for His Faithfulness

Ezra 3:10-13
Timing—536 BC

Praise   Psalm 126:3-4

"The LORD has done great things for us, and we are filled with joy.
  Restore our fortunes, LORD, like streams in the Negev."

Read   Ezra 3:10-13

"When the builders laid the foundation of the temple of the LORD, the priests in their vestments and with trumpets, and the Levites (the sons of Asaph) with cymbals, took their places to praise the LORD, as prescribed by David king of Israel. 11 With praise and thanksgiving they sang to the LORD:
"He is good; his love toward Israel endures forever."
And all the people gave a great shout of praise to the LORD, because the foundation of the house of the LORD was laid. 12 But many of the older priests and Levites and family heads, who had seen the former temple, wept aloud when they saw the foundation of this temple being laid, while many others shouted for joy. 13 No one could distinguish the sound of the shouts of joy from the sound of weeping, because the people made so much noise. And the sound was heard far away."

With the foundation of the Temple completely rebuilt, it was time to focus on praising the Lord for His great faithfulness in the same way David prescribed in I Chronicles 16:1-36. Along with the praise, Ezra 3:12-13 adds that "many of the older priests and Levites and family heads, who had seen the former temple, wept aloud when they saw the foundation of this temple being laid."

During our spiritual journey, we will have both rejoicing and tears as we reflect on God's work. The oldest people were children in Judah before the exile. Compared to this Temple's limited resources, their memories of the magnificent Temple of Solomon overwhelmed them. But God was doing something new and different, as He often does in our lives. As we focus on praise instead of complaining, He will bring His rebuilt and renewed plan into view.

Reflect

• Why were many of the returning exiles praising the Lord?

• As you reflect on your spiritual journey, when have you had times of tears and other times of joy? What brought those feelings to the surface?

Ask the Lord to help you embrace your journey's joys and sorrows.

Yield and kneel to the Lord's sovereignty as He weaves your joy and sorrows.

Your UpRooted Journal to Reflect, Ask, and Yield
After journaling your reflection questions, read/listen to Tiffany's encouraging song about being dreamers on our UpRooted journey.

"We Are the Dreamers" by Tiffany Thompson and Amy Wallace
It may look like we are wasting our lives, but not all who wander are lost
It may look like days are passing us by
But beauty is a flower in need of showers and time

These are the days we're connecting the dots
These are the words that give voice to your thoughts, cause
We are the dreamers, waking and shaking the city that's been sleeping
We are believers, we wake up and shake up the city that's been wasting away

It may look like there are not enough years to heal all the pain
And loosen the chain one link at a time
People say we have all lost our minds
But maybe it takes love to really create love in a life

Guidepost 13—Focus on praising God for His faithfulness.

DAY 14 Guidepost 14—Focus on Gratitude and Songs of Joy

Psalm 126

Timing—537-535 BC

Praise Psalm 126:5

"Those who sow with tears will reap with songs of joy."

Read Psalm 126

"When the LORD restored the fortunes of Zion, we were like those who dreamed.
2 Our mouths were filled with laughter, our tongues with songs of joy.
Then it was said among the nations, "The LORD has done great things for them."
3 The LORD has done great things for us, and we are filled with joy.
4 Restore our fortunes, LORD, like streams in the Negev.
5 Those who sow with tears will reap with songs of joy.
6 Those who go out weeping, carrying seed to sow,
will return with songs of joy, carrying sheaves with them.""

Reflect

- Psalm 126 was our focused praise this week. Reread the words and journal how they embody the emotions of the exiles as they stand at the Temple's foundation, prepared to build it.

- Write down how they acknowledge God's handiwork as the source of their great joy.

Ask the Lord to continue to remind you of His goodness on your spiritual journey toward faith and obedience. Ask for the Lord to reveal His goodness to others.

Yield to the Lord's direction of sowing tears and trusting Him for a harvest of joyful songs.

Your UpRooted Journal to Reflect, Ask, and Yield
Read/listen to Tiffany's song, "Real Joy," as another expression of gratitude toward God. Journal some of your praises of real joy at God's good gifts to you.

"Real Joy" by Tiffany Thompson
I feel the floodgate, I feel my floodgate open
Healing water, the sweetest water, starting to flow
I see the breakers; I see my breakers are crumbling
The mighty river, the holy river coming home
Bringing joy, real joy
Underlining and overwhelming all of me

It's in the quiet, it's in the quiet that I hear
Words so deep, truths so deep, it doesn't disappear
I sense a smile; I sense a smile in the still
The Spirit's moving, healing, restoring a broken world
Bringing joy, real joy, underlining and overwhelming all of me

I found life at the cross, turn around, and pour it out
I found love in Christ, turn around, pour it out
Sharing joy, real joy, underlining and overwhelming
Joy, real joy, it's underlining and overwhelming all of me

DAY 15   Guidepost 15—Focus on Following and Fearing God, not Man

Ezra 4:1-24

Timing—536 BC

Praise   Psalm 126:6

"Those who go out weeping, carrying seed to sow,
will return with songs of joy, carrying sheaves with them."

Read   Ezra 4:1-24

"When the enemies of Judah and Benjamin heard that the exiles were building a temple for the LORD, the God of Israel, 2 they came to Zerubbabel and to the heads of the families and said, "Let us help you build because, like you, we seek your God and have been sacrificing to him since the time of Esarhaddon king of Assyria, who brought us here.""

3 But Zerubbabel, Joshua and the rest of the heads of the families of Israel answered, "You have no part with us in building a temple to our God. We alone will build it for the LORD, the God of Israel, as King Cyrus, the king of Persia, commanded us."

4 Then the peoples around them set out to discourage the people of Judah and make them afraid to go on building. 5 They bribed officials to work against them and frustrate their plans during the entire reign of Cyrus king of Persia (536 BC) and down to the reign of Darius king of Persia (520 BC)."

In verses 6-23, Ezra inserts two examples of letters that show the kind of opposition Israel suffered under the later reigns of the Persian Kings, Xerxes (485-465 BC) and Artaxerxes (465-426 BC). It clarifies that the opposition started about the Temple but continued by the enemies of the Jews who wrote letters to the future kings accusing the Jews of trying to rebuild the city for a rebellious purpose. The mandate by Cyrus was to build the Temple. That was Zerubbabel's and the returning exile's only focus. (Note: The full text of Ezra 4 is in Toolbox on pages 116-117.)

The chapter's last verse, Ezra 4:24, refocuses on the opposition of the enemies at the time of Zerubbabel and Joshua.

"Thus the work on the house of God in Jerusalem came to a standstill until the second year of the reign of Darius king of Persia."

The standstill would last 16 years. They needed a guidepost at this critical juncture: "Focus on following and fearing God, not man."

1. Focus on following God and His plan!

God moved King Cyrus to appoint the exiled Jews to build the Temple. The neighboring people offered to help. But Zerubbabel and Joshua knew their offer's influence and unclear motives would not provide the resources the Lord wanted them to have.

2. Focus on fearing God, not man!

When they started to fear the people, it led to disobedience and discouragement. The Jews felt forced to stop obeying what God called them to do because of the lies presented by their enemies. The civil leader, Zerubbabel, felt this pressure and deep discouragement as the call to rebuild the Temple seemed thwarted.

For sixteen years, the Jews lived around the Temple's foundation and sacrificed at the altar, but they knew their calling was unfinished. Clouds of discouragement overtook the dream of hope that started this journey. What or who would God use to break through this descending darkness?

A time of fear for our family came after eight months of settling in our Moscow apartment. Our Russian landlady decided to take her apartment back. One night, she knocked at the door with her elderly mother and announced they were moving in NOW! She pushed past Rick and headed to our bedroom.

God provided just what we needed during this chaos. While the Lord moved us again, He moved in the hearts of thirty other missionaries to provide:

- Direction—One couple offered their study apartment to store our belongings.
- Resources—Many missionaries and Russians came to help us move everything in two days.
- Challenge—As we left the apartment, our kids said, "We'll have to tell others how God provided for us." After flying to the States for Christmas, we returned to a temporary apartment in Moscow, found a permanent one, and resettled again.

Today's guidepost is essential for us to accomplish the Lord's mission. Focus on following and fearing God, not a man or a hostile landlady.

Reflect
- Journal how and when you faced enemies or challenges that made you want to stop moving toward God's call on your life.

Ask the Lord to give you the strength to face the enemies that seek to detour you from His call.

Yield to following and fearing the Lord instead of distracting enemies.

51

Your UpRooted Journal to Reflect, Ask, and Yield

Read/listen to Tiffany Thompson's song, "Love Set Aside," reflecting on difficult times when you've needed encouragement, like Zerubbabel and Joshua, who tried to build the Temple with such pressure from their enemies. Personal note: Tiffany wrote this song for me during one of my times of discouragement.

"Love's Set Aside" by Tiffany Thompson
You look a bit beat up today
Did their words knock your breath away?
I know you didn't intend to fight
Can I carry the bags underneath your eyes?

You've got no white flag to fly
They took it from us last time
I know they twisted all your words
Now, silence is all you have to say

Though there's smoke rising from ashes
Don't worry now, I set love aside
I see tears falling from your eyes

Leave the lamp, take my hand
The sky is darkest before the dawn
I'll turn your cheek if you'll turn mine
Just believe we'll survive

Come and rest with me, I may be young, but I'm not weak
Come and lay your head on my knee, oh, I care for you, and I won't leave

Guidepost 15—Focus on following and fearing God, not man.

Weeks 1-3 Review
Reflective Questions for Individual and Small Group

1. Why did God have His people go into exile from Judah to Babylon? II Chronicles 36:15-21

2. How did God provide the way for His people to return to Judah after the 70 years of exile in Babylon? Ezra 1-2

3. What was God's primary goal for His people on their return to Judah? How did the people accomplish that goal? Ezra 3

4. What were their highs and lows as they tried to achieve the goal of building the Temple? Ezra 4

During Weeks 4-6, we'll discover two prophetic voices the Lord gave to His people to clarify and challenge them after sixteen years of silence at the Temple's foundation.

Prayers of JOY
(Jesus, Others, You)

Jesus, I'm thankful for

Others' Prayer Needs

Your Prayer Needs

The potency of prayer

has subdued the strength of fire;

it has bridled the rage of lions,

hushed anarchy to rest, extinguished wars,

appeased the elements, expelled demons,

burst the chains of death,

expanded the gates of heaven,

assuaged disease, repelled frauds,

rescued cites from destruction,

stayed the sun in its course,

and arrested the progress of the thunderbolt.

Prayer is an all-efficient panoply,

a treasure undiminished,

a mine which is never exhausted,

a sky unobscured by clouds,

a heaven unruffled by the storm.

It is the Root,

the fountain,

the mother of a thousand blessings.

John Chrysostom

Early church father (347-407 AD)

Introduction to Weeks 4-6
God's Rooting Review for Our UpRooted Journey

Ezra 5:1 begins, "Now Haggai the prophet and Zechariah the prophet, a descendant of Iddo, prophesied to the Jews in Judah and Jerusalem in the name of the God of Israel, who was over them." God breaks through the sixteen years of discouragement and the thundering silence at the Temple foundation through the prophetic duet of Haggai and Zechariah. Both men traveled from Babylon under the leadership of Zerubbabel and Joshua. Now, the Lord moves in them to bring His clarifying call for the people to rebuild the Temple and return to Him!

Chronologically, which means the order of the time of occurrence, the minor prophetic books of Haggai 1-2 and Zechariah 1:1-6 follow the verse of Ezra 5:1. Haggai, the elderly prophet, and Zechariah, the younger prophet, provide this needed review from the Lord—the perfect life coach. For the next 15 days of devotionals, we will journey through four Rooting Reviews God designed for His discouraged, uprooted people. The process offers new insights into what God knows, questions, challenges, directs, and resources His people based on their responses. New pathways are ahead for them to root in their relationship with God in the Promised Land.

Praise Psalm 138 and 139 will be our Praise verses. They are Psalms of David sung by the returning exiles as they journeyed into God's Word and His ways.

Read

Week	Theme	Timing	Scriptures	Page
		520 BC		
Week 4	God's 1st Rooting Review on God's Timing			59
		6th month	Ezra 5:1	
			Haggai 1	
Week 5	God's 2nd Rooting Review on God's Plan			73
		7th month	Haggai 2:1-9	
	God's 3rd Rooting Review on God's Call		Zechariah 1:1-6	78
		8th month		
	God's 4th Rooting Review on God's Word (Part 1)			82
			Haggai 2:10-19	
Week 6	God's 4th Rooting Review on God's Word (Part 2)			87
		9th month	Haggai 2:20-23	
	God's Rooting Reviews Applied		Ezra 5:2-6:22	90
		516 BC		
Conclusion	ReRooting by God's Designed			103

> **God provides Rooting Reviews through Haggai and Zechariah.**

The occasion of fear

furnishes us with

the occasion of obedience.

Elizabeth Elliot

When I am afraid,

I put my trust in you.

In God, whose word I praise—

In God I trust and am not afraid.

What can mere mortals do to me?

Psalm 56: 3-4

Week 4 God's 1st Rooting Review—God's Timing

Ezra 5:1, Haggai 1

The fear of the neighbor's accusations and possible collaboration with the new Persian leadership caused Zerubbabel, Joshua, and all Jews to stop building the Temple. What was the focus of their lives during the sixteen-year delay? Ezra 5:1 announces a prophetic duet to this post-exilic stage. The one singing base is Haggai, an elderly Jew exiled to Babylon 70 years before as a young man. Zechariah, a young man born in Babylon, sings tenor with a message of boldness and strength.

As we meditate through Haggai 1, we'll see how God reveals His people's sixteen-year fruitless path. Then, we'll see how He guides their thinking with a Rooting Review process. Haggai is so aware of the divine origin of his messages that he affirms the divine authority by saying, "This is what the LORD Almighty says:" twenty-five times throughout his two chapters. In *The Unfolding Drama of Redemption*, W. Graham Scroggie says of Haggai and Zechariah, "God does not allow the conscience of His people to disintegrate. When we are in danger of a fatal coma, He rouses us by some challenging voice and starts us once more on the path of duty."

Praise Psalm 138 was a song of the returning remnant.

Rooting Ideas After journeying through Day 16-20 devotionals, take the time to review the reflective questions at the end of the week. Progressively, fill-in the Prayer Page of JOY (Jesus, Others, You).

Read

Day	*Theme*	*Timing—520 BC*	*Scriptures*	*Page*
	God's #1 Rooting Review—God's Timing			
Day 16	God Knows		Haggai 1:1-2	60
Day 17	God Questions		Haggai 1:3-4	62
Day 18	God Challenges		Haggai 1:5-6	64
Day 19	God Directs		Haggai 1: 7-11	66
Day 20	Our Response God Resources		Haggai 1:12-15	68

Week 4 Review—Reflective Questions for Individual and Small Group 71

God's Rooting Reviews are for our good and His glory!

Day 16 God's 1ˢᵗ Rooting Review—God Knows   Haggai 1:1-2
Timing—520 BC, 6ᵗʰ month, 1ˢᵗ day

Praise Psalm 138:1
"I will praise you, LORD, with all my heart; before the "gods" I will sing your praise."

Read Haggai 1:1-2
"In the second year of King Darius, on the first day of the sixth month, the word of the LORD came through the prophet Haggai to Zerubbabel son of Shealtiel, governor of Judah, and to Joshua son of Jozadak, the high priest: 2 This is what the LORD Almighty says: "These people say, 'The time has not yet come to rebuild the LORD's house.'""

The goal of a life coach is to help you clarify goals, identify obstacles, and surface strategies to overcome problems. The Lord of Life is the perfect Life Coach seeking to root His people in His will and their joy. The Rooting Review process developed in the four sermons of Haggai 1-2, and Zechariah 1:1-6 offers progressive insights into what God knows, questions, challenges, directs, and resources His people based on their response.

Haggai 1:1 sets the timeline as the second year of Persian King Darius (520 BC) in the sixth month and first day. Sixteen years passed since the returning Jews rebuilt the altar area, cleared the foundation, and planned to begin rebuilding the Temple. The Lord starts with a clarifying fact in the form of what He knows as He guides His people toward recovery, strength, and obedience.

Reflect
Jot down from Haggai 1:1-2 what God Knows about the situation of His people.
- **God Knows**
  - God knows—When?
  The exact year, month, and day He came to Haggai to speak His mind to His people in the second year of the new Persian King Darius in the sixth month and the first day of the year. It is comforting that our God knows every detail!

  - God knows—Who needs to hear His Words in this passage?

  - God knows—What are they thinking?

Ask the Lord to reveal what He knows and what you need to hear from Him.

Yield to the Lord's all-knowing understanding about your life.

Your UpRooted Journal to Reflect, Ask, and Yield
Reflect on the prayer below as you meditate and journal on what God knows about your present timing and thinking.

From *Valley of Vision-a collection of Puritan Prayers & Devotions*
"The Awakened Sinner" (Page 36)
O my forgetful soul,
Awake from thy wandering dream;
    turn from chasing vanities,
    look inward, forward, upward,
    view thyself,
    reflect upon thyself,
        who and what thou art, why here,
        what thou must soon be.
Thou art a creature of God,
    formed and furnished by him,
    lodge in body like a shepherd in his tent;
    dost thou not desire to know God's ways?

> **God's 1st Rooting Review—God knows our wrong thinking.**

Day 17   God's 1ˢᵗ Rooting Review—God Questions   Haggai 1:3-4
Timing—520 BC, 6ᵗʰ month, 1ˢᵗ day

Praise   Psalm 138:2

"I will bow down toward your holy temple and will praise your name for your unfailing love and your faithfulness, for you have so exalted your solemn decree that it surpasses your fame."

Read   Haggai 1:3-4

"Then the word of the LORD came through the prophet Haggai:
4 "Is it a time for you yourselves to be living in your paneled houses,
while this house remains a ruin?"

Our Praise verse states the Lord exalts His solemn decree or word. We see that in Haggai 1:3, "Then the word of the LORD came." The last prophet God spoke through before Haggai was Daniel during the seventy years of the Babylonian exile. Then, He moved King Cyrus to call His people to return to Jerusalem and build His temple. But for sixteen years, the silence of the Temple work echoed the silence of God's voice. Then, the word of the Lord came through the prophet Haggai. In verse 4, the Lord, as their life coach, asks His silenced people a soul-searching question. "Is it a time for you yourselves to be living in your paneled houses, while this house remains a ruin?"

They had come from years of basic comforts in Babylon. The challenge of their return and resettling was to lead to the hard work of rebuilding God's Temple. After the pushback by their enemies, they turned their goal to gathering personal comforts. That will never be the Lord's intent for His people. He wants us to be rooted but not self-centered with a self-serving agenda. Haggai is God's megaphone to help awaken them from their spiritual lethargy. *The Gospel in Haggai* by Sacra Script Ministries states, "We live in a world that focuses on meeting our own desires and offers God the leftovers."

Reflect

Jot down from Haggai 1:3-4 What God Questions about the situation.

- **God Questions**
  - God Questions—Who?

  - God Questions—What?

  - God Questions—Timing?

Ask the Lord to reveal His questions to you and others about His priorities for your lives.

Yield to the Lord's questions about your life situations.

Your UpRooted Journal to Reflect, Ask, and Yield
Read/listen to Tiffany's song, "One Voice," as you reflect on God's questions to
you today with a heart that listens.

"One Voice" by Tiffany Thompson, Joshua Silverberg, Aaron Morgan
I'm listening for your heartbeat
But it's noisy on this city street
I'm searching for open doors
But bright lights keep blinding me

I fall to ground with empty hands
I long for the sound
So come on, call me in

One Voice, One Voice
It's all I want, it's all I want to hear
Is Your Voice, Your Voice
Loud and clear

Would I miss it if I fell asleep?
Would I notice if it rang through my dreams?
But if You were to pass me by
Would I even recognize?
Or fall to the ground with empty hands
I long for the sound, so come on in, call me in

Can You cut through the noise?
If you breathe, I'll sing
And if you speak, I'm listening

God's 1st Rooting Review—God questions us and our detours.

Day 18 God's 1st Rooting Review—God Challenges　　Haggai 1:5-6

Timing—520 BC, 6th month, 1st day

Praise　Psalm 138:3
"When I called, you answered me; you greatly emboldened me."

Read　Haggai 1:5-6
"Now this is what the LORD Almighty says: "Give careful thought to your ways.
6 You have planted much, but harvested little. You eat, but never have enough.
You drink, but never have your fill. You put on clothes, but are not warm.
You earn wages, only to put them in a purse with holes in it.""

The challenge: "Give careful thought to your ways." After sixteen years of choosing inverted priorities, the Lord clarified He knows and questions their way of thinking and choices to not move ahead with the building of the Temple. In verses 5-6, He challenges them to carefully evaluate their priorities on planting, eating, drinking, clothing, and earning wages. He wisely adds the negative consequences of their wrong priorities. Can you hear God saying, "If it is time to serve your own needs and not fulfill My call on your life, have you taken time to observe whether you have My blessing or not?"

Reflect
- **God Challenges**

Jot down how God Challenges His people.
   o   What is His primary challenge to them? To you?

   o   What realms of their lives does He challenge them to give serious reflection? To you?

Ask the Lord to help you and others see any lack of His blessing based on wrong priorities.

Yield to His challenge to give careful thought to your ways.

Your UpRooted Journal to Reflect, Ask, and Yield
Read/listen to Tiffany's song, "Let It Break Through," as you consider the Lord's challenge to Zerubbabel, Joshua, His people, and you—journal about your challenges and how He desires to break through your thinking with His Heaven's light.

"Let It Break Through" by Tiffany Thompson and Chris Franz
You were always the stronger one
Meant to be king and collide with setting suns
I always knew you'd find a home in the hearts of children, men, and stone
Brave enough to lead a charge and never let the weakest one fall

But the winds at your back
Turned and attacked
Dragging us down slow
Let it break through, let it break you
Don't you ever fear your heart is lost
Heaven's light, you can trust
To break through

Your golden hour faded quick
Thought you had it all, but what's a crown when you don't pay for it
I know you've been brought to your knees, but now you can rest
Let the tears heal your eyes, let the ache throb in your chest

Let it break through, let it break you
If you ever fail to weigh the cost
Heaven's light you can trust
To break through
So let the love, precious love, trapped in your lungs

God's 1st Rooting Review—God challenges us to review and make corrections.

DAY 19 God's 1ˢᵗ Rooting Review—God Directs   Haggai 1:7-11
Timing—520 BC, 6ᵗʰ month, 1ˢᵗ day

Praise Psalm 138:4
"May all the kings of the earth praise you, LORD, when they hear what you have decreed."

Read   Haggai 1:7-11
7 "This is what the LORD Almighty says: "Give careful thought to your ways.
8 Go up into the mountains and bring down timber and build my house,
so that I may take pleasure in it and be honored," says the LORD.
9 "You expected much, but see, it turned out to be little. What you brought home, I blew away. Why?" declares the LORD Almighty. "Because of my house, which remains a ruin, while each of you is busy with your own house.
10 Therefore, because of you the heavens have withheld their dew and the earth its crops.
11 I called for a drought on the fields and the mountains, on the grain, the new wine, the olive oil and everything else the ground produces, on people and livestock, and on all the labor of your hands."

In verses 7-8, the Lord directs them to consider their ways carefully. Then, He directs their thinking toward clear steps of obedience to bring His call and their lives into alignment.
    "Go up into the mountains and bring down timber and BUILD MY HOUSE."

In Ezra chapters 3 and 4, they quit building His house out of fear of their enemies. Instead of constructing His Temple when trouble came, they used the timber to erect their houses to please themselves. After His clear directions, the Lord gives His desired purpose behind completing His Temple in verse 8.
        "So that I may take pleasure in it and be honored."

In verse 9, their Life Coach provides this Rooting Review in case of brain fog.
        "You expected much, but see, it turned out to be little.
            What you brought home, I blew away.
        "WHY?" declares the LORD Almighty.
        "Because of my house, which remains a ruin,
            while each of you is busy with your own house."

In verses 10-11, He directs them to own and confess the negative impact of their bad choices. "Therefore, because of you the heavens have withheld their dew and the earth its crops. I called for a drought on the fields and the mountains, on the grain, the new wine, the olive oil and everything else the ground produces, on people and livestock, and on all the labor of your hands."

The Lord calls us out of a worldly focus to His narrative and agenda. He calls us to live with different priorities while the world's sirens call us away from Him.

Reflect

- **God Directs**

Highlight in today's verses how God is directing His people toward clear steps of obedience.

  o   How is the Lord directing you to "Give careful thought to your ways?"

Ask the Lord to help you and others see His clear and blessed steps of direction.

Yield to the direction the Lord speaks to your heart and mind today.

Your Uprooted Journal to Reflect, Ask, and Yield
Read/listen to Tiffany's lyrics as the Lord calls to your heart.

"Take It and Run" by Tiffany Thompson and Chris Franz
You've had days of laughing in the sun
But this isn't one, no, this isn't one
It feels like you're missing out,
Love's let you down, and your heart is running dry
Come on, come on, hold your head up high

You've got too much now to throw it all away?
You've got to give up all that ails you, tomorrow is on its way
You've got to look back here and see how far you've come
Take in this minute and all that you've been given and run
Come on, come on, take what you've been given and run

Do you feel you're the only one
With dreams and doubt, who's going to fall fighting it out?
Yeah, you'd give anything for a winning streak
Hold on, I know you're going to find a way

Breathe deep, it's a new day
It's going to take time, and it's OK if you're afraid
You need to reach deep where the hope hides and bring it back to life

God's 1ˢᵗ Rooting Review—God directs us toward clear steps of obedience.

Day 20 God's 1ˢᵗ Rooting Review—Our Response/God Resources

Haggai 1:12-15
Timing—520 BC, 6ᵗʰ month, 24th day

Praise Psalm 138:5

"May they sing of the ways of the LORD, for the glory of the LORD is great."

Read Haggai 1:12-15

"Then Zerubbabel son of Shealtiel, Joshua son of Jozadak, the high priest, and the whole remnant of the people obeyed the voice of the LORD their God and the message of the prophet Haggai, because the LORD their God had sent him. And the people feared the LORD.

13 Then Haggai, the LORD's messenger, gave this message of the LORD to the people: "I am with you," declares the LORD.

14 So the LORD stirred up the spirit of Zerubbabel son of Shealtiel, governor of Judah, and the spirit of Joshua son of Jozadak, the high priest, and the spirit of the whole remnant of the people. They came and began to work on the house of the LORD Almighty, their God, 15 on the twenty-fourth day of the sixth month."

Reflect

• **Our Response**—Jot down all the "What should be our response?" insights that you observe in these verses.

• **God Resources**—Jot down the "What resources will God provide?" insights you observe in these verses.

First, the Lord provided His Rooting Review process for His people through His prophet, Haggai—God Knows, Questions, Challenges, and Directs. Then, the leaders, Zerubbabel and Joshua, the high priest, and the whole remnant of the people obeyed the voice of the Lord their God and the message of the prophet Haggai because the Lord their God had sent him. The Lord knows we have limitations to see through the fog of our sin and disobedience. So, if we are willing to be guided by His Rooting Reviews and go to His Word to hear what He knows, listen to His questions, and accept His challenges and direction for our lives, we will find the blessings He longs to give of us.

In Haggai 1:12b, "And the people feared the Lord" was the response of all the people. Along with their obedience, a renewed understanding of the fear of God came upon the whole remnant. In my book, *Rooted Woman of Valor*, I teach about the Proverbs 31 woman's fear of God heart. I developed an acrostic with the word FEAR to help define and remember what it means to fear God from all the verses of Scripture that have that phrase.

> **F**orsake—leave behind, put off
> **E**vil—everything that God says is sin and disobedience
> **A**cknowledge God in everything, agree with His wisdom and will
> **R**everence Him in your heart and worship

We see that obedience to God comes from a fear of God heart that chooses to forsake the evil and disobedience and acknowledges what the Lord knows, questions, challenges, and takes His direction on the UpRooted spiritual journey.

Ask the Lord to continue His sovereign Rooting Review for you and others seeking to find His will and a blessed life of obedience.

Yield to the Lord with a renewed understanding of what it means to fear Him and obey.

Your UpRooted Journal to Reflect, Ask, and Yield
Journal your response to these questions.

- What response is the Lord asking of you in your situation(s)?

- What resources is He providing through people, Scriptural insight, or direction?

Your UpRooted Journal to Reflect, Ask, and Yield
Read/listen to Tiffany's song, "Band Together," to reflect on the Lord's call to do His will and band with others for His Glory as God's people did in Haggai.

"Band Together" by Tiffany Thompson and Jenn Bostic
We're not made to walk crowded streets alone
People we pass aren't mere steppingstones
We've been told to get there fast
But once we reach the top, the first place never lasts
No, it never lasts

When the whole world crashes down
We're the ones who stick around
Through the stormiest of weather
Working hard to make things better
We go so much farther when we
Band together

We're all seeing a different shade of green
Imagine a future made of every possibility
When we hold what we know too close
We shut the door on what we really want to know

Oh, what a joyful noise! Band together
Oh, what a happiness! Band together
Oh, what a motley crew! Band together
We find the courage to see it through,
Band together

God's 1ˢᵗ Rooting Review— God Resources us when our Response is to have a fear of God heart.

Week 4 Review
Reflective Questions for Individual and Small Group

As you end Week 4 and Haggai 1, focus on that key area in your life
of discouragement or fear this past year.

- Think about the time, the situation, the people involved when you felt the
  farthest away from the Lord, most discouraged, and in need of direction.
- Then, personalize this **God's Rooting Review**.
  (In the Toolbox on pages 108-109, I provide a template of this review for
  you to use as a regular spiritual journey review.

1. **God Knows** (Haggai 1:2)
   You are sitting around thinking it is not time to build the temple now.

2. **God Questions** (Haggai 1:3-4)
   Is it time to build your houses? He asks us questions to help us understand
   our detours.

3. **God Challenges** (Haggai 1:5-7)
   Give careful thought to their ways!

4. **God Directs** (Haggai 1:8-11)
   Go up and build my house!

5. **Our Response** (Haggai 1:12)
   Obedience and renewed understanding of fear of God heart
   > **F**orsake
   > **E**vil
   > **A**cknowledge the Lord in everything
   > **R**everence Him in worship

6. **God Resources** (Haggai 1:13-15)
   His Presence (vs. 13)
   His Empowerment (vs. 14)

Prayers of JOY
(Jesus, Others, You)

Jesus, I'm thankful for

Others' Prayer Needs

Your Prayer Needs

Week 5
God's 2nd Rooting Review—God's Plan   **Haggai 2:1-9**
God's 3rd Rooting Review—God's Call   **Zechariah1:1-6**
God's 4th Rooting Review—God's Word (Part 1) **Haggai 2:10-19**

Timing—520 BC, 7th month, 24th day, the final day of the feast of Tabernacle

By the end of Haggai 1, God's people heard the challenge and direction from God, their Life Coach. Their response was obedience and a renewed fear of God heart. First, He sent the resource of His presence, "I am with you," declares the Lord" (Haggai 1:13b). Next, He sent His empowerment, "So the Lord stirred up the spirit of Zerubbabel son of Shealtiel, governor of Judah, and the spirit of Joshua son of Jozadak, the high priest, and the spirit of the whole remnant of the people" (Haggai 1:14a). They responded in obedience and began working on the Lord Almighty's house in Haggai 1:14. We saw God's Rooting Review pattern that He used to help process their thinking. We will continue to see this process guide His people twice in Haggai 2 and once in Zechariah 1:1-6.

Praise Psalms 138:6-8 and 139:1-2 are by King David sung by the rooting remnant.

Rooting Idea After journeying through Days 21-25 devotionals, take the time to review the reflective questions and Prayers of JOY at the end of the week.

Day	*Theme*	*Timing—520 BC*	*Scriptures*	*Page*
	God's 2nd Rooting Review—God's Plan			
Day 21	God Knows, Questions, Challenges, Directs, and Resources based on Response	Haggai 2:1-5		74
Day 22	God Challenges, Directs, Resources, and Reveals His Plan	Haggai 2:6-9		76
	God's 3rd Rooting Review—God's Call			
Day 23	God Knows, Challenges, and Resources based on Response	Zechariah1:1-4		78
Day 24	God Questions and Resources based on Response	Zechariah 1:5-6		80
	God's 4th Rooting Review—God's Word (Part 1)			
Day 25	God Knows, Questions, Challenges, Directs, and Resources based on Response	Haggai 2:10-19		82
Week 5	Review—Reflective Questions for Individual and Small Group			85

God's 2nd, 3^{rd,} and 4th Rooting Reviews are for His glory and our good!

DAY 21 God's 2nd Rooting Review—God's Plan
God Knows, Questions, Challenges, Directs, and Resources based on Response
Haggai 1:15b; 2:1-5

Timing—520 BC, 7th month, 21st day, Haggai's 2nd message comes 7 weeks after his 1st message in Haggai 1

Praise Psalm 138:6
"Though the LORD is exalted, he looks kindly on the lowly;
though lofty, he sees them from afar."

Read Haggai 1:15b; 2:1-5
1:15b "In the second year of Darius,
2:1 on the twenty-first day of the seventh month, the word of the LORD came through the prophet Haggai: 2 "Speak to Zerubbabel son of Shealtiel, governor of Judah, to Joshua son of Jozadak, the high priest, and to the remnant of the people. Ask them, 3 'Who of you is left who saw this house in its former glory? How does it look to you now? Does it not seem to you like nothing? 4 But now be strong, Zerubbabel,' declares the LORD. 'Be strong, Joshua son of Jozadak, the high priest. Be strong, all you people of the land,' declares the LORD, 'and work. For I am with you,' declares the LORD Almighty. 5 'This is what I covenanted with you when you came out of Egypt. And my Spirit remains among you. Do not fear.'"

After rebuilding the Temple for over a month, it was time for the Jewish Feast of Tabernacles. For a week, the Jews celebrated the harvest, presented offerings, and lived in temporary shelters. This annual event was a time to remember God's provision of freedom from Egypt, as described in Leviticus 23. On the last day of the festival, the prophet Haggai, whose name meant festival, spoke forth God's 2nd Rooting Review before the building of the Temple would resume.

Reflect
- **God Knows** it is time to give His leaders and people more direction.
  From Haggai 2:1-2, who is God speaking to?

- **God Questions** "Ask them," from Haggai 2:2b. Fill in each question and the answer God wanted His people to consider from Haggai 2:3.
  ○ Question 1 Who?

  ○ Question 2 How?

  ○ Question 3 Does?

  ○ How do these questions relate to this house in its former glory?
     Who built the first glorious Jewish Temple? (2 Chronicles 2:1)

The Lord's questions surfaced the problem of an internal discouragement sweeping over His people's efforts to build the Temple. As Ezra 3:12,13 said, the older Jews remembered the magnificent Temple in Jerusalem that Nebuchadnezzar destroyed because, as children, they saw it before their captivity. As they worked on rebuilding the Temple, the realization that it could never compare brought tears and negative talk that ensued a cloud of discouragement. God's rooting review challenged them to refocus their questions on correct thinking and actions.

- **God Challenges** (Haggai 2:4) What are the two specific challenges?

- **God Directs** (Haggai 2:4) What is the right **Response**/action?

- **God Resources**
  o (Haggai 2:4) What does He offer as His Resource?

  o (Haggai 2:5) What Resource from their history does He remind them of?

Ask the Lord to clarify the above Rooting Review process for your situation.

Yield your spirit and memory to the Lord and ask for His divine perspective.

Your UpRooted Journal to Reflect, Ask, and Yield
Take time to process an area of discouragement through God's Rooting Review.

God Knows   What and who does God know about your situation?

God Questions   What is God asking you?

God Challenges   How is God challenging you?

God Directs   How is God directing you?

God Resources   What is God providing for you?

God's 2ⁿᵈ Rooting Review—God Knows, Questions, Directs, and Resources based on our Response as He reveals His Plan.

Day 22   God's 2nd Rooting Review—God's Plan
God Challenges, Directs, Resources, and Reveals His Plan   Haggai 2:6-9
Timing—520 BC, 7th month, 21st day, Haggai's 2nd message 7 weeks after 1st

Praise   Psalm 138:7
"Though I walk in the midst of trouble, you preserve my life. You stretch out your hand against the anger of my foes; with your right hand you save me."

Read   Haggai 2:6-9
6"This is what the LORD Almighty says: 'In a little while I will once more shake the heavens and the earth, the sea and the dry land. 7 I will shake all nations, and what is desired by all nations will come, and I will fill this house with glory,' says the LORD Almighty. 8 'The silver is mine and the gold is mine,' declares the LORD Almighty. 9 'The glory of this present house will be greater than the glory of the former house,' says the LORD Almighty. 'And in this place, I will grant peace,' declares the LORD Almighty."

God heard the questions of His complaining, fearful people. He reveals His challenge, direction, and resources to explain His plans. Isaiah 55:8 reminds us, "For my thoughts are not your thoughts, neither your ways my ways."
- **Challenge of God's Plan** (Haggai 2:6)
"In a little while I will once more shake the heavens and the earth, the sea and dry land." God's "little while" would be 500 years. In 2 Peter 3:8-9a, the Lord reminds us, "But do not forget this one thing, dear friends: With the LORD a day is like a thousand years, and a thousand years are like a day. The LORD is not slow in keeping his promise, as some understand slowness." The shakings and earthquakes are symbols of God's supernatural interventions.
- **Direction of God's Plan** (Haggai 2:7)
"I will shake all nations and what is desired by all nations will come, I will fill this house with glory.' says the LORD Almighty." His question to the leaders and remnant in Haggai 2:3 was, "Does this Temple seem to you like nothing?" But in 2:7, He clarifies the direction of His plan for this rebuilt Temple. It is the arrival of "What is desired by all nations will come, and I will fill this house with glory." Jesus, as the God/man, filled this Temple with glory, beginning in Luke 2 when Joseph and Mary took Jesus to present him before the Lord. Simeon took Jesus in his arms and praised God, saying: "Sovereign Lord, as you have promised, …your salvation, which you have prepared in the sight of all nations: a light for revelation to the Gentiles, and the glory of your people Israel" (Luke 2:28-32).
- **Resources of God's Plan** (Haggai 2:8)
"'The silver is mine and the gold is mine,' declares the Lord Almighty." The remnant focused on their lack of resources compared to King Solomon's day. The Lord reminds them that all the silver, gold, and everything is His. He chose to provide what they needed for His calling on their lives at this time and place. Did they forget that He had heathen nations store and return the original Temple treasures to be placed in this Temple they were building?

- **Revelation of God's Plan** (Haggai 2:9)

"'The glory of this present house will be greater than the glory of the former house,' says the LORD Almighty. 'And in this place, I will grant peace,' declares the LORD Almighty."

The final clarification is for everyone to focus on the goal of building the Temple and not complain or give into fear. In *Notes on the Minor Prophets*, H.A. Ironside explains, "Not only had they the Lord's presence, in Spirit with them, but His coming in person was to be their hope."

Reflect

Process your present fears and complaints through the Lord's Rooting Review.

God Challenges Us—How is God challenging your fears and complaints?

God Directs Us—How is God directing you through this passage?

Our Response—What should your response be as you consider these insights?

God Resources—What resources will God provide?

Ask the Lord to continue to help you bring your life's fears and complaints into His coaching as you seek Him through His Word.

Yield to the Lord's Life Coaching for you today!

Your UpRooted Journal to Reflect, Ask, and Yield

God's 2ⁿᵈ Rooting Review—God Challenges, Directs, Resources, and reveals His Plan.

Day 23   God's 3rd Rooting Review—God's Call

God Knows, Challenges, and Resources based on Response

Zechariah 1:1-4

Timing:520 BC, 8th month

Praise   Psalm 138:8

"The LORD will vindicate me; your love, LORD, endures forever—
do not abandon the works of your hands."

Read   Zechariah 1:1-4

"In the eighth month of the second year of Darius, the word of the LORD came to
the prophet Zechariah son of Berekiah, the son of Iddo:
2 "The LORD was very angry with your ancestors.
3 Therefore tell the people: This is what the LORD Almighty says: 'Return to me,'
declares the LORD Almighty, 'and I will return to you,' says the LORD Almighty.
4 Do not be like your ancestors, to whom the earlier prophets proclaimed: This is
what the LORD Almighty says: 'Turn from your evil ways and your evil practices.'
But they would not listen or pay attention to me, declares the LORD."

Haggai's first two Rooting Review messages focus on what God Knows,
Questions, Challenges, Directs, and Resources His people. The goal was to guide
them to be strong, work, and focus on Him instead of fear and complaining. About
ten days passed, and the Lord brought the voice of Zechariah, the younger of the
post-exilic prophetic duet. He prophesied a short, strong message in the 8th month,
encompassing only the first six verses of his book of fourteen chapters and 31
years of ministry from 520-489 BC. We know Zechariah's message comes
between Haggai's four messages because of the timing in Zechariah 1:1. (520 BC
is the date of all these messages.)

See how the Lord uses His Rooting Review again in Zechariah's message.
*   **God Knows** (Zechariah 1:1)
"In the eighth month of the second year of Darius, the word of the LORD came to
the prophet Zechariah son of Berekiah, the son of Iddo."
God knows everyone's name and its meaning.
Zechariah means 'Jehovah Remembers.'
Berekiah means 'Jehovah blesses.' Iddo means 'at the appointed time.'
Summary—God remembers and blesses at the appointed time.

*   **God Knows** (Zechariah 1:2)
"The LORD was very angry with your ancestors."
He knows our ancestors, those who came before us, and their relationship
to Him.

(**God Questions** Note: The questions come at the end of Zechariah's message in
verses 5-6).

- **God Challenges and Directs** (Zechariah 1:3)
"Therefore tell the people: This is what the LORD Almighty says: 'Return to me,' declares the LORD Almighty." His challenge and directions are for the people to 'Return to Me.'

Our Response (Zechariah 1:4)
"Do not be like your ancestors, to whom the earlier prophets proclaimed: This is what the LORD Almighty says: 'Turn from your evil ways and your evil practices.' But they would not listen or pay attention to me, declares the LORD."
God reminds them of their ancestors' response and warns them not to respond to Him as they did. The correct response is listening, paying attention to the Lord, and turning from their evil practices.

- **God Resources** (Zechariah 1:3b)
"'Return to me,' declares the LORD Almighty, 'and I will return to you,' says the LORD Almighty." The Lord gives room for us to return to Him, then He will return to us. When we feel He is far away and uninterested in our lives, He is very close and ready for us to draw near.

Reflect
Journal your response below to God's Rooted Review in Zechariah. Do you need to return to Him? James 4:8 reminds us, "Come near to God and he will come near to you."

Ask the Lord to help you come near to Him.

Yield to His clear and loving direction to return into His arms.

Your UpRooted Journal to Reflect, Ask, and Yield

God's 3rd Rooting Review— God Knows, Challenges, and Resources based on our Response to His Call.

Day 24   God's 3ʳᵈ Rooting Review—God's Call

God Questions and Resources based on Response   Zechariah 1:5-6

Timing:520 BC, 8ᵗʰ month

Praise   Psalm 139:1

"You have searched me, LORD, and you know me."

Read   Zechariah 1:5-6

5 "Where are your ancestors now? And the prophets, do they live forever?
6 But did not my words and my decrees, which I commanded my servants the prophets, overtake your ancestors? "Then they repented and said, 'The LORD Almighty has done to us what our ways and practices deserve, just as he determined to do.'"

- **God Questions Us** (Zechariah 1:5-6)

First, the Lord coaches them through His Rooting Review of what He Knows, Challenges, Directs, and Resources in His message through Zechariah. Then, He provides Rooting Review Questions for them to reflect on their generational past so they will not fall into the same evil patterns that led to their ancestors' exile. What are the obvious answers to God's questions?

   o   "Where are your ancestors now?" (5a)

   o   "And the prophets, do they live forever?" (5b)

   o   "But did not my words and my decrees, which I commanded my servants the prophets, overtake your ancestors?" (6a)

- **Our Response** (Zechariah 1:6)

"Then they repented and said, 'The LORD Almighty has done to us what our ways and practices deserve, just as he determined to do.'"

Returning and repenting allow for a pure heart to draw near to God. Hebrews 10:22 reminds us, "Let us draw near to God with a sincere heart and with the full assurance that faith brings, having our hearts sprinkled to cleanse us from a guilty conscience and having our bodies washed with pure water."

- **God's Resources** (stated earlier in Zechariah 1:2b)

"'Return to me,' declares the LORD Almighty, 'and I will return to you,' says the LORD Almighty." After Haggai's first two messages, God's people obeyed by building the Temple. Zechariah's short but strong message speaks to the deeper heart issue, essential to move one's obedience to the soul level. God seeks to guide us to abide in His love and peace. He wants a reciprocal relationship with us. He is always close and calls us to move toward Him.

Reflect

To help us live and move toward God and His call of obedience, He has given us this pattern in Haggai and Zechariah 1:1-6 as a Rooting Review for Personal Reflection. Take it periodically to help you recognize detours from His loving path. Flow through each question and journal any present detours that tempt you not to stay close to the Lord. (Templates for copying are in the Toolbox on pages 108-109).

1. What does God <u>Know</u> about the situation/problem that He wants me to see?

2. What <u>Question</u>(s) is God asking me about this situation/problem?

3. What <u>Challenge</u>(s) or warning(s) is God giving me to clarify His pathway and perspective?

4. What specific <u>Direction</u>(s) is God giving me through His Word and others?

5. What <u>Response(s)</u> is God asking of me?

6. What <u>Resource(s)</u> is God providing for this situation/problem?

Ask the Lord how He is calling you to return to Him.

Yield to the insights the Lord reveals through your spiritual journey inventory.

Your UpRooted Journal to Reflect, Ask, and Yield

God's 3rd Rooting Review— God Questions and Resources based on our Response to His Call.

Day 25 God's 4th Rooting Review—God's Word (Part 1)
God Knows, Questions, Challenges, Directs, and Resources based on Response

Haggai 2:10-19

Timing: December 18, 520 BC, 9th month, 24th day

Praise   Psalm 139:2
"You know when I sit and when I rise; you perceive my thoughts from afar."

Read   Haggai 2:10-19
"On the twenty-fourth day of the ninth month, in the second year of Darius, the word of the LORD came to the prophet Haggai: 11 "This is what the LORD Almighty says: 'Ask the priests what the law says: 12 If someone carries consecrated meat in the fold of their garment, and that fold touches some bread or stew, some wine, olive oil or other food, does it become consecrated?' "
The priests answered, "No."
13 Then Haggai said, "If a person defiled by contact with a dead body touches one of these things, does it become defiled?" "Yes," the priests replied, "it becomes defiled."
14 Then Haggai said, "'So it is with this people and this nation in my sight,' declares the LORD. 'Whatever they do and whatever they offer there is defiled.
15 "'Now give careful thought to this from this day on—consider how things were before one stone was laid on another in the LORD's temple. 16 When anyone came to a heap of twenty measures, there were only ten. When anyone went to a wine vat to draw fifty measures, there were only twenty. 17 I struck all the work of your hands with blight, mildew and hail, yet you did not return to me,' declares the LORD.
18 'From this day on, from this twenty-fourth day of the ninth month, give careful thought to the day when the foundation of the LORD's temple was laid. Give careful thought: 19 Is there yet any seed left in the barn? Until now, the vine and the fig tree, the pomegranate and the olive tree have not borne fruit.
"'From this day on I will bless you.'"

- **God Knows** (Haggai 2:10)

After Zechariah's 'Return to Me' challenge, about a month flew by as they continued building the Temple. Then, Haggai brought the next step in the Rooting Review. God knows the people need a deeper lesson on returning to Him and how it relates to rebuilding the Temple.

- **God Questions** (Haggai 2:11-14)

Now, the Lord addresses the priests about ceremonial cleansing.
1. Does a consecrated (holy) item make everything it touches holy? NO
This issue relates to the ritual of sin offering of Leviticus. 6:24-27.
2. Does a defiled item make everything that it touches defiled? YES! God speaks to the issue of the heart. Even though they are working hard on it, the Temple itself will not make them holy. Only He, as the holy God, can make them holy.

David Levy's commentary, *When Prophets Speak of Judgment,* clarifies, "The Mosaic Law taught that moral cleanness cannot be transmitted but moral uncleanness can. The same is true in physical life. Health between people cannot be transferred, but sickness can. Israel had originally been set apart for the Lord's use. The exile was a time of cleansing for the land, now they needed to return to Him to be made holy again. Disobedience leads to uncleanliness that leads to Divine blessing withheld. Face it: God doesn't wink at sin!"

- **God Answers the Questions** (Haggai 2:14)

Then Haggai said, "'So it is with this people and this nation in my sight,' declares the LORD. 'Whatever they do and whatever they offer there is defiled.'" Note: God refers to 'this people', not 'my people'.

They needed to repent and return from the heart to be pure before Him.

- **God Challenges** (Haggai 2:15-17)

"'Now give careful thought to this from this day on—consider how things were before one stone was laid on another in the LORD's temple. 16 When anyone came to a heap of twenty measures, there were only ten. When anyone went to a wine vat to draw fifty measures, there were only twenty. 17 I struck all the work of your hands with blight, mildew and hail, yet you did not return to me,' declares the LORD."

God provides His review of their past 16 years by clarifying that the lack of blessing was rooted in His displeasure about the state of their prodigal hearts.

- **God Directs** (Haggai 2:18-19)

"'From this day on, from this twenty-fourth day of the ninth month, give careful thought to the day when the foundation of the LORD's temple was laid. Give careful thought: 19 Is there yet any seed left in the barn? Until now, the vine and the fig tree, the pomegranate and the olive tree have not borne fruit." The Lord directs the nation—"consider from this day forward."

He directs them to stop and turn toward Him in obedience. As 2 Corinthians 6:2b says, "I tell you, now is the time of God's favor, now is the day of salvation."

- **Our Response** (Haggai 2:15, 18)

"Give careful thought to your ways."

We must return to God. Stop going our way and choose Him and His shepherding path.

- **God Resources** (Haggai 2:19b)

"'From this day on I will bless you.'"

The Lord loves our movement of returning to Him. He knows that on that very day, He will bless us. What a Shepherd He is!

Reflect

With the issue of sincerely returning in our hearts to obey the Lord and receive His blessing in our lives, reflect on what the Lord is asking you to do "From this day forward." Journal below.

Ask the Lord to continue revealing your heart's true condition.

Yield to the Lord's challenge to return to Him from this day forward!

Your Uprooted Journal to Reflect, Ask, and Yield
Read Tiffany's song, "Dirty Wings," and journal where your heart is with the Lord today. (It is not on playlist.)

"Dirty Wings" by Tiffany Thompson, Paul Mabry, and Paul Duncan
Fowl, I fly to the fountain
Find a breeze beneath my dirty wings
Turn my gaze to the mountain
A valley full of sirens sings to me, Come and see

Lost, I look for the lighthouse
A little girl used to know the way
Do I head for home or a hideout?
A host of smiling saviors call my name, Come and see

Pretty little chains to hold me
The glory of the now unfolding over me
Fire rises from an ember
A thousand steps to one surrender calling
Come and see, Come and see, Come and see

Fowl, I fly to the fountain
Find a breeze beneath my dirty wings

God's 4ᵗʰ Rooting Review—God Knows, Questions, Challenges, Directs, and Resources based on our Response to His Word.

Week 5 Review
Reflective Questions for Individual and Small Group

1. **Praise** What praise verse was your favorite this week? Why?

2. **Read** What Scriptural insight challenged you the most this week?

3. **Reflect** What were some of your reflections in your UpRooted Journal?

4. **Ask** What are you asking the Lord to do in your life and others this week?

5. **Yield** How is the Lord working in your life to yield to His promptings?

6. What **guidepost** are you making and taking with you this week?

Prayers of JOY
(Jesus, Others, You)

Jesus, I'm thankful for

Others' Prayer Needs

Your Prayer Needs

Week 6 God's 4th Rooting Review—God's Word (Part 2) Haggai 2:20-23
God's Rooting Reviews Applied   Ezra 5-6

Recap of the timing and focus of Haggai and Zechariah's messages:
6th month: Haggai—God's Timing to start building the Temple
7th month: Haggai—God's Plan for the Temple's future
8th month: Zechariah—God's Call to return to Him
9th month: Haggai—God's Word on the need for purity of heart

God's 4th Rooting Review (Part 2) is His Word to His appointed leader, Zerubbabel. After Haggai's final message, we will head back to Ezra 5-6 to see the impact on the history of this period and what happened because of God's Rooting Reviews through Haggai and Zechariah. Did the messages speak to their hearts and transform their faith and actions?

Praise Psalm 139:3-12 is a song of the remnant as they begin to reroot.

Rooting Idea After journeying through Day 26-30 devotionals, take the time to review with reflective questions at the end of the week. They are good to use for a small group study. Progressively, fill-in the Prayer Page of JOY (Jesus, Others, You) located after the Review page.

Day	Theme	Timing	Scriptures	Page
		520 BC		
	God's 4th Rooting Review—God's Word (Part 2)			
Day 26	God Knows and Directs		Haggai 2:20-23	88
	God's Rooting Reviews Applied			
Day 27	God Questions to Reveal Lessons		Ezra 5:1-17	90
Day 28	God Resources Abundantly		Ezra 6:1-12	93
Day 29	God Directs toward Obedience		Ezra 6:13-18	96
Day 30	ReRooting by God Designed		Ezra 6:19-22	98

Week 6 Review—Reflective Questions for Individual or Small Group   100

God's Rooting Reviews are for His glory and our good!

Day 26 God's 4th Rooting Review—God's Word (Part 2) Haggai 2:20-23
>
> God Knows and Directs   *Timing: December 18, 520 BC, 9th month 24th day, (2nd time)*

Praise   Psalm 139:3-4
"You discern my going out and my lying down; you are familiar with all my ways. Before a word is on my tongue you, LORD, know it completely."

Read   Haggai 2:20-23
"The word of the LORD came to Haggai a second time on the twenty-fourth day of the month:
21 "Tell Zerubbabel governor of Judah that I am going to shake the heavens and the earth.
22 I will overturn royal thrones and shatter the power of the foreign kingdoms. I will overthrow chariots and their drivers; horses and their riders will fall, each by the sword of his brother.
23 "'On that day,' declares the LORD Almighty, 'I will take you, my servant Zerubbabel son of Shealtiel,' declares the LORD, 'and I will make you like my signet ring, for I have chosen you,' declares the LORD Almighty."

The final Rooting Review lesson is for Zerubbabel, the central leader of the remnant. It will provide the clarity and encouragement he needs to lead God's people courageously during the new surge of rebuilding the Temple.

- **God Knows** (Haggai 2:22) the leader's thinking.

The Lord speaks directly to Zerubbabel as the governor. For 16 years, he chose not to lead the rebuilding of the Temple because of his fear of kings and enemies. God reminds His leader to focus on who He is, His future, and His sovereign plan of victory, whether the shattering of foreign kingdoms happens in his generation or not. Zerubbabel lived by faith without seeing this happen in his lifetime. Hebrews 11:13,16 says, "All these people were still living by faith when they died. They did not receive the things promised; they only saw them and welcomed them from a distance, admitting that they were foreigners and strangers on earth…longing for a better country—a heavenly one."

- **God Directs** (Haggai 2:21) His word to the leader—
  "Tell Zerubbabel governor of Judah."

God directs his hope to be in His sovereign plans, not their problems. In verse 23, the word 'that' day refers to future fulfillment. Here, Zerubbabel is not called the governor but my servant. My servant is a term used for the coming Messiah throughout Isaiah 40-55. In Matthew 1, we find the genealogy of the Messiah, born 500 years later. God's sovereign plan included his servant Zerubbabel, as seen in Matthew 1:12, "After the exile to Babylon: Jeconiah was the father of Shealtiel, Shealtiel the father of Zerubbabel." Matthew 1:17 summarizes, "Thus there were fourteen generations in all from Abraham to David, fourteen from David to the exile to Babylon, and fourteen from the exile to the Messiah."

2. Zerubbabel is challenged to trust God's redemptive plan, not his failure.

Haggai 2:23 ends with this prophetic blessing on Zerubbabel, "And I will make you like my signet ring, for I have chosen you,' declares the LORD Almighty." A signet ring was used by kings or authorities to stamp its impression on important documents. Though Zerubbabel came from the kingly line of Judah, he was not a king on his return from exile. In Jeremiah 22:24-25, God sends this word to his grandfather, the last king of Judah before the exile, "As surely as I live," declares the LORD, "even if you, Jehoiachin son of Jehoiakim king of Judah, were a signet ring on my right hand, I would still pull you off. I will deliver you into the hands of those who want to kill you, those you fear—Nebuchadnezzar king of Babylon and the Babylonians." In verse 22:30b, it states, "for none of his offspring will prosper, none will sit on the throne of David or rule anymore in Judah."

But God sees in this fearful grandson a pure and fear of God heart. He chose Zerubbabel as His signet ring for this returning people to leave a godly impression of the Lord Almighty. With renewed purpose and faith, Zerubbabel and all the people humbly and courageously began to rebuild the Temple.

Reflect on the Lord's call and chosen ministry for your life.
- o What impression does He want you to have on the world?

- o What promise is He asking you to believe by faith, whether you see it here or in heaven?

Ask the Lord to give you the wisdom, courage, and redemption that He offered Zerubbabel as you face the challenges of leading others in your realm of influence. Pray for your civic and church leaders.

Yield to the Lord's chosen plan for you to be His signet ring to leave a godly impression.

Your UpRooted Journal to Reflect, Ask, and Yield

God's 4th Rooting Review—God knows and directs.

Day 27 God's Rooting Reviews Applied—
God Questions to Reveal Lessons   Ezra 5:1-17
Timing:520 BC, 9th month

Praise Psalm 139:5-6
"You hem me in behind and before, and you lay your hand upon me.
Such knowledge is too wonderful for me, too lofty for me to attain."

Read Ezra 5:1-17   Rebuilding and More Challenges
1 "Now Haggai the prophet and Zechariah the prophet, a descendant of Iddo,
prophesied to the Jews in Judah and Jerusalem in the name of the God of Israel,
who was over them.

(Note: Ezra 5:2-6:22 finish the rest of the history of these returning exiles after
the prophetic messages of Haggai and Zechariah 1:1-6. Sheshbazzar is another
name for Zerubbabel in the letter to the Persian King Darius.)

2 Then Zerubbabel son of Shealtiel and Joshua son of Jozadak set to work to
rebuild the house of God in Jerusalem. And the prophets of God were with them,
supporting them.
3 At that time Tattenai, governor of Trans-Euphrates, and Shethar-Bozenai and
their associates went to them and asked, "Who authorized you to rebuild this
temple and to finish it?" 4 They also asked, "What are the names of those who are
constructing this building?" 5 But the eye of their God was watching over the
elders of the Jews, and they were not stopped until a report could go to Darius and
his written reply be received.
6 This is a copy of the letter that Tattenai, governor of Trans-Euphrates, and
Shethar-Bozenai and their associates, the officials of Trans-Euphrates, sent to
King Darius.
7 The report they sent him read as follows:
To King Darius: Cordial greetings.
8 The king should know that we went to the district of Judah, to the temple of the
great God. The people are building it with large stones and placing the timbers in
the walls. The work is being carried on with diligence and is making rapid
progress under their direction.
9 We questioned the elders and asked them, "Who authorized you to rebuild this
temple and to finish it?" 10 We also asked them their names, so that we could
write down the names of their leaders for your information.
11 This is the answer they gave us:
"We are the servants of the God of heaven and earth, and we are rebuilding the
temple that was built many years ago, one that a great king of Israel built and
finished. 12 But because our ancestors angered the God of heaven, he gave them
into the hands of Nebuchadnezzar the Chaldean, king of Babylon, who destroyed
this temple and deported the people to Babylon.
13 "However, in the first year of Cyrus king of Babylon, King Cyrus issued a
decree to rebuild this house of God.

14 He even removed from the temple of Babylon the gold and silver articles of the house of God, which Nebuchadnezzar had taken from the temple in Jerusalem and brought to the temple in Babylon. Then King Cyrus gave them to a man named Sheshbazzar, whom he had appointed governor, 15 and he told him, 'Take these articles and go and deposit them in the temple in Jerusalem. And rebuild the house of God on its site.'

16 "So this Sheshbazzar came and laid the foundations of the house of God in Jerusalem. From that day to the present it has been under construction but is not yet finished."

17 Now if it pleases the king, let a search be made in the royal archives of Babylon to see if King Cyrus did in fact issue a decree to rebuild this house of God in Jerusalem. Then let the king send us his decision in this matter."

In Ezra's historical account of what happened after the prophetic messages of Haggai and Zechariah, the work of God in His people is already evident. We will continue to use the Rooting Review pattern to dig into Ezra 5-6.
As we continue to investigate the Scriptures, we will apply Jeremiah 31:21.
"Set up road signs; put up guideposts.
Take note of the highway, the road that you take.
Return, Virgin, Israel, return to your towns."

Reflect
Use God's Rooting Review to observe insights from this passage.
Read the observations provided and add your own.
- **God Knows**
  - (Ezra 5:5) God knows everything that happens. "But the eye of their God was watching over the elders of the Jews."
  -
- **God Questions** (or Questions from others and answers given)
  - (Ezra 5:3b) "Who authorized you to rebuild this temple and to finish it?"
  - (Ezra 5:4) "They also asked, "What are the names of those who are constructing this building?"
  - (Ezra 5:11,12) When asked by their enemies who authorized the rebuild and their names, they knew who they were: "We are the servants of the God of heaven and earth, and we are rebuilding the temple that was built many years ago and finished."
    They owned their history: "But because our ancestors angered the God of heaven, he gave them into the hands of Nebuchadnezzar the Chaldean, king of Babylon, who destroyed this temple and deported the people to Babylon."
- **God Challenges**
  - (Ezra 5:2-5) The same challenges came from their enemies. What is their response now? They continue to obey even though their enemies try to cause more fear.

- **God Directs**
  - ○ (Ezra 5:13) Confirmation of the truth about their commission and other details occurs through the official letter to the new King Darius.
  - ○

- **Our Response**
  - ○ (Ezra 5:2) All the leaders, prophets, and people set to obey and build the Temple.
  - ○ (Ezra 5:8) The Jews carried on the work diligently and with rapid progress.
  - ○
- **God Resources**
  - ○ (Ezra 5:5) They were not stopped by their enemies while waiting for King Darius' response. They continued building the Temple because "the eye of their God was watching over the elders of the Jews." They obeyed, and God protected them.
  - ○

Ask the Lord to help you and others know that His eye is always upon you.

Yield to the Lord's call on your life today to obey during challenges and uncertainty.

Your UpRooted Journal to Reflect, Ask, and Yield
The lyrics in this song speak to the new conviction of God's people even though fear resurfaces.

"Fear Is Not My Future"
written by Brandon Lake, Hannah Shackleford, Jonathan Jay, Nicole Hannel
Let Him turn it in your favor, Watch Him work it for your good
He's not done with what He's started, no, He's not done until it's good
Hello peace, Hello joy, Hello love, Hello strength, Hello hope, it's a new horizon

If you're ready for a breakthrough, just open up and just receive
'Cause what He's pouring out is nothing you've ever seen
Fear is not my future, You are
Sickness is not my story, You are
Heartbreak is not my home, You are
Death is not the end, You are
You are, You are

God's Rooting Reviews Applied—God Questions to reveal lessons.

Day 28 God's Rooting Reviews Applied—
God Resources Abundantly
Ezra 6:1-12
Timing— 520 BC

Praise Psalm 139:7-8
"Where can I go from your Spirit? Where can I flee from your presence?
If I go up to the heavens, you are there; if I make my bed in the depths,
you are there."

Read Ezra 6:1-12 The Decree of Darius
1 "King Darius then issued an order, and they searched in the archives stored in
the treasury at Babylon. 2 A scroll was found in the citadel of Ecbatana in the
province of Media, and this was written on it:

Memorandum:

3 In the first year of King Cyrus, the king issued a decree concerning the temple
of God in Jerusalem:
Let the temple be rebuilt as a place to present sacrifices, and let its foundations be
laid. It is to be sixty cubits (90 feet) high and sixty cubits wide, 4 with three
courses of large stones and one of timbers. The costs are to be paid by the royal
treasury. 5 Also, the gold and silver articles of the house of God, which
Nebuchadnezzar took from the temple in Jerusalem and brought to Babylon, are
to be returned to their places in the temple in Jerusalem; they are to be deposited
in the house of God.

6 Now then, Tattenai, governor of Trans-Euphrates, and Shethar-Bozenai and you
other officials of that province, stay away from there. 7 Do not interfere with the
work on this temple of God. Let the governor of the Jews and the Jewish elders
rebuild this house of God on its site.
8 Moreover, I hereby decree what you are to do for these elders of the Jews in the
construction of this house of God:
Their expenses are to be fully paid out of the royal treasury, from the revenues of
Trans-Euphrates, so that the work will not stop. 9 Whatever is needed—young
bulls, rams, male lambs for burnt offerings to the God of heaven, and wheat, salt,
wine and olive oil, as requested by the priests in Jerusalem—must be given them
daily without fail, 10 so that they may offer sacrifices pleasing to the God of
heaven and pray for the well-being of the king and his sons.
11 Furthermore, I decree that if anyone defies this edict, a beam is to be pulled
from their house and they are to be impaled on it. And for this crime their house
is to be made a pile of rubble. 12 May God, who has caused his Name to dwell
there, overthrow any king or people who lifts a hand to change this decree or to
destroy this temple in Jerusalem.
I Darius have decreed it. Let it be carried out with diligence."

Reflect
Use God's Rooting Review to observe insights from this passage. There are many verses on God Resources. Read the observations provided and add your own.
Use Your UpRooted Journal to add thoughts of gratitude on how God Resources you abundantly.

- **God Knows**
    o (Ezra 6:2) God knew exactly where the documents were and the protection, they would provide for rebuilding His Temple.
    o (Ezra 6:12b) "I Darius have decreed it." God knew what king would assist the Jews like King Cyrus did.
- **God Questions**
    o
    o
- **God Challenges**
    o (Ezra 6:11) Through King Darius, God warned their neighbors to help with the Temple or die.
    o
- **God Directs**
    o
    o
- **Our Response**
    o
    o
- **God Resources**
    o (Ezra 6:4) Finances- "The costs are to be paid by the royal treasury."
    o (Ezra 6:6) Protection-Enemies told to "stay away from there." (7) "Do not interfere with the work on this temple of God."
    o (Ezra 6:8) Finances- "Their expenses are to be fully paid out of the royal treasury, from the revenues of Trans-Euphrates, so that the work will not stop."
    o (Ezra 6:9-10) "Whatever is needed—young bulls, rams, male lambs for burnt offerings to the God of heaven, and wheat, salt, wine and olive oil, as requested by the priests in Jerusalem—must be given them daily without fail, 10 so that they may offer sacrifices pleasing to the God of heaven and pray for the well-being of the king and his sons."
    o (Ezra 6:11) Protection- "Furthermore, I decree that if anyone defies this edict, a beam is to be pulled from their house and they are to be impaled on it. And for this crime their house is to be made a pile of rubble."
    o (Ezra 6:12) Protection- "May God, who has caused his Name to dwell there, overthrow any king or people who lifts a hand to change this decree or to destroy this temple in Jerusalem."

Ask the Lord to provide reminders of His will, direction, and providential care for you and others.

Yield to His amazing provisions from the most unlikely places, even your enemies.

Your *UpRooted Journal to Reflect, Ask, and Yield*

God's Rooting Reviews Applied— God Resources us abundantly!

Day 29 God's Rooting Reviews Applied—
God Directs toward Obedience   Ezra 6:13-18
Timing:516 BC, 3rd day of the month of Adar, 6th year of King Darius

Praise Psalm 139:9-10
"If I rise on the wings of the dawn, if I settle on the far side of the sea,
even there your hand will guide me, your right hand will hold me fast."

Read   Ezra 6:13-18   Completion and Dedication of the Temple
"Then, because of the decree King Darius had sent, Tattenai, governor of Trans-
Euphrates, and Shethar-Bozenai and their associates carried it out with diligence.
14 So the elders of the Jews continued to build and prosper under the preaching
of Haggai the prophet and Zechariah, a descendant of Iddo. They finished building
the temple according to the command of the God of Israel and the decrees of
Cyrus, Darius and Artaxerxes, kings of Persia.
15 The temple was completed on the third day of the month Adar, in the sixth year
of the reign of King Darius.
16 Then the people of Israel—the priests, the Levites and the rest of the exiles—
celebrated the dedication of the house of God with joy.
17 For the dedication of this house of God they offered a hundred bulls, two
hundred rams, four hundred male lambs and, as a sin offering for all Israel, twelve
male goats, one for each of the tribes of Israel.
18 And they installed the priests in their divisions and the Levites in their groups
for the service of God at Jerusalem, according to what is written in the Book of
Moses.

Reflect
Use God's Rooting Review to observe insights from this passage.
Read the observations provided and add your own.

- **God Knows**
  - (Ezra 6:13) The impact King Darius' decree would have. "Then, because
    of the decree King Darius had sent, Tattenai, governor of Trans-
    Euphrates, and Shethar-Bozenai and their associates carried it out with
    diligence." Their enemies became the resource.☺
  -
- **God Questions**
  -
  -
- **God Challenges**
  - (14) "So the elders of the Jews continued to build and prosper under
    their preaching of Haggai the prophet and Zechariah." God would
    continue to use His prophets to provide challenges and directions.
- **God Directs**
  - (14) His continued direction is seen in the obedience of His people.

- **Our Response**
  - (Ezra 6:14) To obey God's vision to rebuild the temple and enjoy relief from their enemy's pressure.
    "So the elders of the Jews continued to build and prosper under the preaching and of Haggai and Zechariah, a descendant of Iddo. They finished building the temple according to the command of God of Israel and the decree of Cyrus, Darius and Artaxerxes, kings of Persia."
  - (Ezra 6:16) To dedicate the Temple to the Lord. "Then the people of Israel—the priests, the Levites and the rest of the exiles—celebrated the dedication of the house of God with joy."
  - (Ezra 6:17) To follow the sacrificial laws. "For the dedication of this house of God they offered a hundred bulls, two hundred rams, four hundred male lambs and, as a sin offering for all Israel, twelve male goats, one for each of the tribes of Israel."
  - (Ezra 6:18) To install the priests and Levites. "And they installed the priests in their divisions and the Levites in their groups for the service of God at Jerusalem, according to what is written in the Book of Moses."
  -

- **God Resources**
  - (Ezra 6:13,17) All their needs for their Jewish sacrifices for the dedication in verse 17 were provided by the leaders King Darius had appointed in verse 13. Ezra 6:9-10 was the decree. "Whatever is needed—young bulls, rams, male lambs for burnt offerings to the God of heaven, and wheat, salt, wine and olive oil, as requested by the priests in Jerusalem—must be given them daily without fail, so that they may offer sacrifices pleasing to the God of heaven and pray for the well-being of the king and his sons."
  -

Ask the Lord to help you see His abundant provisions and rejoice by worshipping Him.

Yield to the Lord's call on your life, and be amazed at how He will answer and bless you.

Your UpRooted Journal to Reflect, Ask, and Yield

God's Rooting Reviews Applied—God Directs us toward obedience.

Day 30   ReRooting by God's Designed   Ezra 6:19-22
Timing: 516 BC, 1ˢᵗ month, 14ᵗʰ day

Praise   Psalm 139:11-12
"If I say, "Surely the darkness will hide me and the light become night around me," even the darkness will not be dark to you; the night will shine like the day, for darkness is as light to you."

Read   Ezra 6:19-22   The Passover
"On the fourteenth day of the first month, the exiles celebrated the Passover.
20 The priests and Levites had purified themselves and were all ceremonially clean. The Levites slaughtered the Passover lamb for all the exiles, for their relatives the priests and for themselves. 21 So the Israelites who had returned from the exile ate it, together with all who had separated themselves from the unclean practices of their Gentile neighbors in order to seek the Lord, the God of Israel. 22 For seven days they celebrated with joy the Festival of the Unleavened Bread, because the Lord had filled them with joy by changing the attitude of the king of Assyria so that he assisted them in the work of the house of God, the God of Israel."

Reflect
Use God's Rooting Review to observe insights from this passage.
- **God Knows**
  - (Ezra 6:19) The Temple would be finished during Passover.
- **God Questions**
  -
- **God Challenges**
  - (Ezra 6: 21) They were to separate themselves from the unclean practices of their Gentile neighbors.
- **God Directs**
  -
- **Our Response**
  - (Ezra 6:19) After finishing the Temple, they celebrated the Passover and purified themselves.
  - (Ezra 6:22) They celebrated the Festival of Unleavened Bread because the Lord had filled them with joy by changing the attitude of the King of Assyria so that he assisted them in the work on the house of God, the God of Israel.
- **God Resources**
  - (Ezra 6:22) It was clear that the Lord filled them with joy by changing the attitude of the King of Assyria. They knew their God alone resourced all the details to finish the Temple.

The biblical account of the returning exiles *UpRooted by God's Design* ends. But Zerubbabel's name resurfaces in Matthew and Luke's genealogies of Jesus the Messiah. This obedient generation rerooted in Judah and rebuilt the Temple where the Messiah would be born, minister, and die for the world's sins.

May our generation leave an eternal signet ring impression for the Glory of God.

Ask the Lord to make you a part of an obedient generation for His glory.

Yield to the Lord's call on your life to make His impression on this generation.

Your UpRooted Journal to Reflect, Ask, and Yield
Read/listen to Tiffany's song, "Soul of the Nation." Reflect on how God rerooted His people to become the godly soul of His nation.

"Soul of the Nation" by Tiffany Thompson and Jenn Bostic
Let it be said, when we finish this race
We kept them free, we led with grace
Let it be seen, from sea to shining sea,
Beautiful Promised Land, living our legacy

O, father, mother, sister, brother,
O, we've got to learn to love each other
O, for the soul of the nation
O, for the next generation

Let us be known, as people of honor
Humble and bold, faithful through fire
Let us hold firm, to our convictions
With wide open hearts, eager to listen

Let us make room, let us reimagine
Welcoming voices, with true compassion
Let's craft a world, with hopes and dreams
For challenges known, and those still unseen

Let us be sure when our time has come
We gave them hope, we made them strong
Let it be said, when we finish this race
We kept them free, we led with grace

God's Rooting Reviews Applied—ReRooting begins by God's design!

Week 6 Review
Reflective Questions for Individual and Small Group

1. **Praise** What praise verse was your favorite this week? Why?

2. **Read** What Scriptural insight challenged you the most this week?

3. **Reflect** What were some of your reflections in your UpRooted Journal?

4. **Ask** What are you asking the Lord to do in your life and others this week?

5. **Yield** How is the Lord working in your life to yield to His promptings?

6. What **guidepost** are you making and taking with you this week?

Prayers of JOY
(Jesus, Others, You)

Jesus, I'm thankful for

Others' Prayer Needs

Your Prayer Needs

Conclusion
ReRooting by God's Design

We have taken the spiritual journey through Ezra 1-6, Haggai 1-2, and Zechariah 1:1-6. We watched the uprooted remnant return to the Lord by faith and obedience. We observed the God-given Guideposts along the way. God's eye watched over them as they moved from fear to faith. We learned a Rooting Review pattern the Lord, our Life Coach, uses that is a resource for our future Bible study and application.

God Knows, God Questions, God Challenges,
God Directs, Our Response, and God Resources

We saw the Lord remove every obstacle as they fulfilled their calling to rebuild the Temple and glorify Him. By God's design and grace, the exiles moved from an UpRooted people to a people beginning to ReRoot in the Promised Land and their God.

This Jewish remnant and their two prophets, Haggai and Zechariah, made a significant stroke on the magnificent mural that the Lord Almighty is designing of Truth, Redemption, Righteousness, Providence, Provision, and Prophecy as His plan for man, the world, and future kingdom unfold. With the Temple rebuilt, the prophecy of Haggai 2:6,7 readied itself for the fulfillment of Jesus entering its doors 500 years later. Jesus came to that Temple, died for our sins, arose, and returned to heaven.

This is what the LORD Almighty says:
'In a little while I will once more shake the heavens
and the earth, the sea and the dry land.
I will shake all nations,
and what is desired by all nations
will come,
and I will fill this house with glory,'
says the LORD Almighty.

Haggai 2:6,7

Jesus Christ will come back again!

He who testifies to these things says,
"Yes, I am coming soon."
Amen.
Come, Lord Jesus.

Revelation 22:20

Toolbox

for

UpRooted
by God's Design

UpRooted by God's Design
Template

Daily, Doable, Deep Devotional—3D Plan
(**P**raise, **R**ead/**R**eflect, **A**sk, **Y**ield)

Praise

Read

Reflect

Ask

Yield

Your UpRooted Journal to Reflect, Ask, and Yield

UpRooted by God's Design
Template

Prayers of JOY
(Jesus, Others, You)

Jesus, I'm thankful for

Others' Prayer Needs

Your Prayer Needs

UpRooted by God's Design
Template

God's Rooting Review for Personal Reflection

Based on Haggai and Zechariah 1:1-6.
Use for a monthly spiritual journey review.

"Set up road signs; put up guideposts.
Take note of the highway, the road that you take.
Return, Virgin, Israel, return to your towns."

Jeremiah 31:21

1. What does God <u>Know</u> about the situation/problem that He wants me to see?

2. What <u>Question</u>(s) is God asking me about this situation/problem?

3. What <u>Challenge</u>(s) or warning(s) is God giving me to clarify His pathway and perspective?

4. What specific <u>Direction</u>(s) is God giving me through His Word and others?

5. What <u>Response(s)</u> is God asking of me?

6. What <u>Resource(s)</u> is God providing for this situation/problem?

UpRooted by God's Design
Template

God's Rooting Review for Personal Reflection

Based on Haggai and Zechariah 1:1-6.
Use for a monthly spiritual journey review.

"Set up road signs; put up guideposts.
Take note of the highway, the road that you take.
Return, Virgin, Israel, return to your towns."

Jeremiah 31:21

1. What does God <u>Know</u> about the situation/problem that He wants me to see?

2. What <u>Question</u>(s) is God asking me about this situation/problem?

3. What <u>Challenge</u>(s) or warning(s) is God giving me to clarify His pathway and perspective?

4. What specific <u>Direction</u>(s) is God giving me through His Word and others?

5. What <u>Response(s)</u> is God asking of me?

6. What <u>Resource(s)</u> is God providing for this situation/problem?

Timeline Chart
for Ezra, Haggai, and Zechariah 1:1-6

BC

1050-1010	King Saul reign over Israel (40 years)	1 Samuel 12
1010-970	King David reign over Israel (40 years)	2 Samuel 2
970-940	King Solomon reign over Israel (40 years)	1 Kings 2-3
970-960	Solomon builds the Temple	1 Kings 2-9
960-586	Solomon's 1st Temple exists	
930-722	Israel divides into northern and southern kingdoms	
722	The northern kingdom falls to Assyria	2 Kings 17
627	Time of Daniel's birth in Judah before the exile	
607	Babylonian captivity begins in time of Jehoiakim	Daniel 1:1-6
		2 Chronicles 36:6-7
605	First siege on Jerusalem	2 Kings 25
	First wave of exiles captured	Jeremiah 52:28-30
		2 Chronicles 36:5-8
597	Second siege on Jerusalem and the capture of King Jehoiachin	
		2 Chronicles 36:10
586	Third siege on Jerusalem/Destruction of the Temple and city	
	Nebuchadnezzar carries the Temple's treasures to Babylon	
	with the rest of the exiles	2 Chronicles 36:17-19
539	Cyrus the Persian conquers Babylon	2 Chronicles 36:20-21
538	First year of Cyrus II ruling Babylon	2 Chronicles 36:22-23
	He issues edict that Jews can return to Jerusalem	
	to build the Temple	
538	Zerubbabel and Joshua lead 50,000 exiles to Judah	Ezra 1-2
537	Daniel prospers under King Cyrus	Daniel 6:28
536	Exiles first year in Judah	Ezra 3
535	Altar and foundation of the Temple begins	
530-522	Persian King Cambyses	
522-486	Persian King Darius I	
522	Temple construction stopped by opposition	Ezra 4
520	Prophet Haggai and Prophet Zechariah	Haggai 1, 2
	God's Word to start building the Temple again	Zechariah 1
520	Rebuilding of Temple Resumes	Ezra 5:2-6
516	Temple Finished and Dedicated	
486-465	Persian King Xerxes I,	
473	Esther is Queen of Persia	
465-425	Persian King Artaxerxes	
458	Second exile group returns to Jerusalem,	Ezra 7-10
	(90 years since Zerubbabel's group) Ezra reforms synagogues	
445	Third exile group returns with Nehemiah	
	Nehemiah rebuilds the walls of Jerusalem.	
440-430	Books of Ezra, Nehemiah, and Malachi written,	
	then 400 years of silence until Jesus Christ's birth	

110

Chronological Bible Text of
Ezra 1-6, Haggai, and Zechariah 1:1-6

Ezra 1   Cyrus Helps the Exiles to Return

¹ In the first year of Cyrus king of Persia, in order to fulfill the word of the LORD spoken by Jeremiah, the LORD moved the heart of Cyrus king of Persia to make a proclamation throughout his realm and also to put it in writing:

² "This is what Cyrus king of Persia says:

"'The LORD, the God of heaven, has given me all the kingdoms of the earth and he has appointed me to build a temple for him at Jerusalem in Judah. ³ Any of his people among you may go up to Jerusalem in Judah and build the temple of the LORD, the God of Israel, the God who is in Jerusalem, and may their God be with them. ⁴ And in any locality where survivors may now be living, the people are to provide them with silver and gold, with goods and livestock, and with freewill offerings for the temple of God in Jerusalem.'"

⁵ Then the family heads of Judah and Benjamin, and the priests and Levites— everyone whose heart God had moved—prepared to go up and build the house of the Lord in Jerusalem. ⁶ All their neighbors assisted them with articles of silver and gold, with goods and livestock, and with valuable gifts, in addition to all the freewill offerings.

⁷ Moreover, King Cyrus brought out the articles belonging to the temple of the LORD, which Nebuchadnezzar had carried away from Jerusalem and had placed in the temple of his god. ⁸ Cyrus king of Persia had them brought by Mithredath the treasurer, who counted them out to Sheshbazzar the prince of Judah.

⁹ This was the inventory:

gold dishes	30
silver dishes	1,000
silver pans	29
¹⁰ gold bowls	30
matching silver bowls	410
other articles	1,000

¹¹ In all, there were 5,400 articles of gold and of silver. Sheshbazzar brought all these along with the exiles when they came up from Babylon to Jerusalem.

Ezra 2   The List of the Exiles Who Returned

[1] Now these are the people of the province who came up from the captivity of the exiles, whom Nebuchadnezzar king of Babylon had taken captive to Babylon (they returned to Jerusalem and Judah, each to their own town, [2] in company with Zerubbabel, Joshua, Nehemiah, Seraiah, Reelaiah, Mordecai, Bilshan, Mispar, Bigvai, Rehum and Baanah):

The list of the men of the people of Israel:

[3] the descendants of Parosh	2,172
[4] of Shephatiah	372
[5] of Arah	775
[6] of Pahath-Moab (through the line of Jeshua and Joab)	2,812
[7] of Elam	1,254
[8] of Zattu	945
[9] of Zakkai	760
[10] of Bani	642
[11] of Bebai	623
[12] of Azgad	1,222
[13] of Adonikam	666
[14] of Bigvai	2,056
[15] of Adin	454
[16] of Ater (through Hezekiah)	98
[17] of Bezai	323
[18] of Jorah	112
[19] of Hashum	223
[20] of Gibbar	95
[21] the men of Bethlehem	123
[22] of Netophah	56
[23] of Anathoth	128
[24] of Azmaveth	42
[25] of Kiriath Jearim, Kephirah and Beeroth	743
[26] of Ramah and Geba	621
[27] of Mikmash	122
[28] of Bethel and Ai	223
[29] of Nebo	52
[30] of Magbish	156
[31] of the other Elam	1,254
[32] of Harim	320

[33] of Lod, Hadid and Ono 725
[34] of Jericho 345
[35] of Senaah 3,630

[36] The Priests:

the descendants of Jedaiah (through the family of Jeshua) 973
[37] of Immer 1,052
[38] of Pashhur 1,247
[39] of Harim 1,017

[40] The Levites:

the descendants of Jeshua and Kadmiel 74
(of the line of Hodaviah)

[41] The musicians:

the descendants of Asaph 128

[42] The gatekeepers of the temple:

the descendants of
Shallum, Ater, Talmon,
Akkub, Hatita and Shobai 139

[43] The temple servants:

the descendants of
Ziha, Hasupha, Tabbaoth,
[44] Keros, Siaha, Padon,
[45] Lebanah, Hagabah, Akkub,
[46] Hagab, Shalmai, Hanan,
[47] Giddel, Gahar, Reaiah,
[48] Rezin, Nekoda, Gazzam,
[49] Uzza, Paseah, Besai,
[50] Asnah, Meunim, Nephusim,
[51] Bakbuk, Hakupha, Harhur,
[52] Bazluth, Mehida, Harsha,
[53] Barkos, Sisera, Temah,
[54] Neziah and Hatipha

113

[55] The descendants of the servants of Solomon:

the descendants of
Sotai, Hassophereth, Peruda,
[56] Jaala, Darkon, Giddel,
[57] Shephatiah, Hattil,
Pokereth-Hazzebaim and Ami

[58] The temple servants and the descendants of the servants of Solomon   392

[59] The following came up from the towns of Tel Melah, Tel Harsha, Kerub, Addon and Immer, but they could not show that their families were descended from Israel:

[60] The descendants of
Delaiah, Tobiah and Nekoda 652

[61] And from among the priests:

The descendants of
Hobaiah, Hakkoz and Barzillai (a man who had married a daughter of Barzillai the Gileadite and was called by that name).

[62] These searched for their family records, but they could not find them and so were excluded from the priesthood as unclean. [63] The governor ordered them not to eat any of the most sacred food until there was a priest ministering with the Urim and Thummim.

[64] The whole company numbered 42,360, [65] besides their 7,337 male and female slaves; and they also had 200 male and female singers. [66] They had 736 horses, 245 mules, [67] 435 camels and 6,720 donkeys.

[68] When they arrived at the house of the LORD in Jerusalem, some of the heads of the families gave freewill offerings toward the rebuilding of the house of God on its site. [69] According to their ability they gave to the treasury for this work 61,000 darics of gold, 5,000 minas of silver and 100 priestly garments.

[70] The priests, the Levites, the musicians, the gatekeepers and the temple servants settled in their own towns, along with some of the other people, and the rest of the Israelites settled in their towns.

Ezra 3 Rebuilding the Altar

[1]When the seventh month came and the Israelites had settled in their towns, the people assembled together as one in Jerusalem. [2]Then Joshua son of Jozadak and his fellow priests and Zerubbabel son of Shealtiel and his associates began to build the altar of the God of Israel to sacrifice burnt offerings on it, in accordance with what is written in the Law of Moses the man of God. [3]Despite their fear of the peoples around them, they built the altar on its foundation and sacrificed burnt offerings on it to the LORD, both the morning and evening sacrifices. [4]Then in accordance with what is written, they celebrated the Festival of Tabernacles with the required number of burnt offerings prescribed for each day. [5]After that, they presented the regular burnt offerings, the New Moon sacrifices and the sacrifices for all the appointed sacred festivals of the LORD, as well as those brought as freewill offerings to the LORD. [6]On the first day of the seventh month they began to offer burnt offerings to the LORD, though the foundation of the LORD's temple had not yet been laid.

Rebuilding the Temple

[7]Then they gave money to the masons and carpenters, and gave food and drink and olive oil to the people of Sidon and Tyre, so that they would bring cedar logs by sea from Lebanon to Joppa, as authorized by Cyrus king of Persia. [8]In the second month of the second year after their arrival at the house of God in Jerusalem, Zerubbabel son of Shealtiel, Joshua son of Jozadak and the rest of the people (the priests and the Levites and all who had returned from the captivity to Jerusalem) began the work. They appointed Levites twenty years old and older to supervise the building of the house of the LORD. [9]Joshua and his sons and brothers and Kadmiel and his sons (descendants of Hodaviah[f]) and the sons of Henadad and their sons and brothers—all Levites—joined together in supervising those working on the house of God.

[10]When the builders laid the foundation of the temple of the LORD, the priests in their vestments and with trumpets, and the Levites (the sons of Asaph) with cymbals, took their places to praise the LORD, as prescribed by David king of Israel. [11]With praise and thanksgiving they sang to the LORD: "He is good; his love toward Israel endures forever." And all the people gave a great shout of praise to the LORD, because the foundation of the house of the LORD was laid. [12]But many of the older priests and Levites and family heads, who had seen the former temple, wept aloud when they saw the foundation of this temple being laid, while many others shouted for joy. [13]No one could distinguish the sound of the shouts of joy from the sound of weeping, because the people made so much noise. And the sound was heard far away.

Ezra 4 Opposition to the Rebuilding

¹ When the enemies of Judah and Benjamin heard that the exiles were building a temple for the LORD, the God of Israel, ² they came to Zerubbabel and to the heads of the families and said, "Let us help you build because, like you, we seek your God and have been sacrificing to him since the time of Esarhaddon king of Assyria, who brought us here."

³ But Zerubbabel, Joshua and the rest of the heads of the families of Israel answered, "You have no part with us in building a temple to our God. We alone will build it for the LORD, the God of Israel, as King Cyrus, the king of Persia, commanded us."

⁴ Then the peoples around them set out to discourage the people of Judah and make them afraid to go on building. ⁵ They bribed officials to work against them and frustrate their plans during the entire reign of Cyrus king of Persia and down to the reign of Darius king of Persia.

Later Opposition Under Xerxes and Artaxerxes

⁶ At the beginning of the reign of Xerxes, they lodged an accusation against the people of Judah and Jerusalem.

⁷ And in the days of Artaxerxes king of Persia, Bishlam, Mithredath, Tabeel and the rest of his associates wrote a letter to Artaxerxes. The letter was written in Aramaic script and in the Aramaic language.

⁸ Rehum the commanding officer and Shimshai the secretary wrote a letter against Jerusalem to Artaxerxes the king as follows:

⁹ Rehum the commanding officer and Shimshai the secretary, together with the rest of their associates—the judges, officials and administrators over the people from Persia, Uruk and Babylon, the Elamites of Susa, ¹⁰ and the other people whom the great and honorable Ashurbanipal deported and settled in the city of Samaria and elsewhere in Trans-Euphrates.

¹¹ (This is a copy of the letter they sent him.)

To King Artaxerxes,

From your servants in Trans-Euphrates:

[12] The king should know that the people who came up to us from you have gone to Jerusalem and are rebuilding that rebellious and wicked city. They are restoring the walls and repairing the foundations.

[13] Furthermore, the king should know that if this city is built and its walls are restored, no more taxes, tribute or duty will be paid, and eventually the royal revenues will suffer. [14] Now since we are under obligation to the palace and it is not proper for us to see the king dishonored, we are sending this message to inform the king, [15] so that a search may be made in the archives of your predecessors. In these records you will find that this city is a rebellious city, troublesome to kings and provinces, a place with a long history of sedition. That is why this city was destroyed. [16] We inform the king that if this city is built and its walls are restored, you will be left with nothing in Trans-Euphrates.

[17] The king sent this reply: To Rehum the commanding officer, Shimshai the secretary and the rest of their associates living in Samaria and elsewhere in Trans-Euphrates:

Greetings. [18] The letter you sent us has been read and translated in my presence. [19] I issued an order and a search was made, and it was found that this city has a long history of revolt against kings and has been a place of rebellion and sedition. [20] Jerusalem has had powerful kings ruling over the whole of Trans-Euphrates, and taxes, tribute and duty were paid to them. [21] Now issue an order to these men to stop work, so that this city will not be rebuilt until I so order. [22] Be careful not to neglect this matter. Why let this threat grow, to the detriment of the royal interests?

[23] As soon as the copy of the letter of King Artaxerxes was read to Rehum and Shimshai the secretary and their associates, they went immediately to the Jews in Jerusalem and compelled them by force to stop.

[24] Thus the work on the house of God in Jerusalem came to a standstill until the second year of the reign of Darius king of Persia.

Ezra 5:1

[1] Now Haggai the prophet and Zechariah the prophet, a descendant of Iddo, prophesied to the Jews in Judah and Jerusalem in the name of the God of Israel, who was over them.

Haggai 1

A Call to Build the House of the Lord

¹ In the second year of King Darius, on the first day of the sixth month, the word of the LORD came through the prophet Haggai to Zerubbabel son of Shealtiel, governor of Judah, and to Joshua son of Jozadak, the high priest:

² This is what the LORD Almighty says: "These people say, 'The time has not yet come to rebuild the LORD's house.'"

³ Then the word of the LORD came through the prophet Haggai: ⁴ "Is it a time for you yourselves to be living in your paneled houses, while this house remains a ruin?"

⁵ Now this is what the LORD Almighty says: "Give careful thought to your ways. ⁶ You have planted much, but harvested little. You eat, but never have enough. You drink, but never have your fill. You put on clothes, but are not warm. You earn wages, only to put them in a purse with holes in it."

⁷ This is what the LORD Almighty says: "Give careful thought to your ways. ⁸ Go up into the mountains and bring down timber and build my house, so that I may take pleasure in it and be honored," says the LORD. ⁹ "You expected much, but see, it turned out to be little. What you brought home, I blew away. Why?" declares the LORD Almighty. "Because of my house, which remains a ruin, while each of you is busy with your own house. ¹⁰ Therefore, because of you the heavens have withheld their dew and the earth its crops. ¹¹ I called for a drought on the fields and the mountains, on the grain, the new wine, the olive oil and everything else the ground produces, on people and livestock, and on all the labor of your hands."

¹² Then Zerubbabel son of Shealtiel, Joshua son of Jozadak, the high priest, and the whole remnant of the people obeyed the voice of the LORD their God and the message of the prophet Haggai, because the LORD their God had sent him. And the people feared the Lord.

¹³ Then Haggai, the LORD's messenger, gave this message of the LORD to the people: "I am with you," declares the LORD. ¹⁴ So the LORD stirred up the spirit of Zerubbabel son of Shealtiel, governor of Judah, and the spirit of Joshua son of Jozadak, the high priest, and the spirit of the whole remnant of the people. They came and began to work on the house of the LORD Almighty, their God, ¹⁵ on the twenty-fourth day of the sixth month.

The Promised Glory of the New House

In the second year of King Darius,

Haggai 2:1-9

[1] on the twenty-first day of the seventh month, the word of the LORD came through the prophet Haggai: [2] "Speak to Zerubbabel son of Shealtiel, governor of Judah, to Joshua son of Jozadak, the high priest, and to the remnant of the people. Ask them, [3] 'Who of you is left who saw this house in its former glory? How does it look to you now? Does it not seem to you like nothing? [4] But now be strong, Zerubbabel,' declares the LORD. 'Be strong, Joshua son of Jozadak, the high priest. Be strong, all you people of the land,' declares the LORD, 'and work. For I am with you,' declares the LORD Almighty. [5] 'This is what I covenanted with you when you came out of Egypt. And my Spirit remains among you. Do not fear.'

[6] "This is what the LORD Almighty says: 'In a little while I will once more shake the heavens and the earth, the sea and the dry land. [7] I will shake all nations, and what is desired by all nations will come, and I will fill this house with glory,' says the LORD Almighty. [8] 'The silver is mine and the gold is mine,' declares the LORD Almighty. [9] 'The glory of this present house will be greater than the glory of the former house,' says the LORD Almighty. 'And in this place I will grant peace,' declares the LORD Almighty."

Zechariah 1:1-6

A Call to Return to the Lord

[1] In the eighth month of the second year of Darius, the word of the LORD came to the prophet Zechariah son of Berekiah, the son of Iddo:

[2] "The LORD was very angry with your ancestors. [3] Therefore tell the people: This is what the LORD Almighty says: 'Return to me,' declares the LORD Almighty, 'and I will return to you,' says the LORD Almighty. [4] Do not be like your ancestors, to whom the earlier prophets proclaimed: This is what the LORD Almighty says: 'Turn from your evil ways and your evil practices.' But they would not listen or pay attention to me, declares the LORD. [5] Where are your ancestors now? And the prophets, do they live forever? [6] But did not my words and my decrees, which I commanded my servants the prophets, overtake your ancestors?

"Then they repented and said, 'The LORD Almighty has done to us what our ways and practices deserve, just as he determined to do.'"

Blessings for a Defiled People

Haggai 2:1-9

[10] On the twenty-fourth day of the ninth month, in the second year of Darius, the word of the LORD came to the prophet Haggai:

[11] "This is what the LORD Almighty says: 'Ask the priests what the law says: [12] If someone carries consecrated meat in the fold of their garment, and that fold touches some bread or stew, some wine, olive oil or other food, does it become consecrated?'" The priests answered, "No." [13] Then Haggai said, "If a person defiled by contact with a dead body touches one of these things, does it become defiled?" "Yes," the priests replied, "it becomes defiled."

[14] Then Haggai said, "'So it is with this people and this nation in my sight,' declares the LORD. 'Whatever they do and whatever they offer there is defiled.

[15] "'Now give careful thought to this from this day on—consider how things were before one stone was laid on another in the Lord's temple.

[16] When anyone came to a heap of twenty measures, there were only ten. When anyone went to a wine vat to draw fifty measures, there were only twenty. [17] I struck all the work of your hands with blight, mildew and hail, yet you did not return to me,' declares the Lord. [18] 'From this day on, from this twenty-fourth day of the ninth month, give careful thought to the day when the foundation of the LORD's temple was laid. Give careful thought: [19] Is there yet any seed left in the barn? Until now, the vine and the fig tree, the pomegranate and the olive tree have not borne fruit.

"'From this day on I will bless you.'"

Zerubbabel the Lord's Signet Ring

[20] The word of the LORD came to Haggai a second time on the twenty-fourth day of the month: [21] "Tell Zerubbabel governor of Judah that I am going to shake the heavens and the earth. [22] I will overturn royal thrones and shatter the power of the foreign kingdoms. I will overthrow chariots and their drivers; horses and their riders will fall, each by the sword of his brother.

[23] "'On that day,' declares the LORD Almighty, 'I will take you, my servant Zerubbabel son of Shealtiel,' declares the LORD, 'and I will make you like my signet ring, for I have chosen you,' declares the LORD Almighty."

Ezra 5   Tattenai's Letter to Darius

[1] Now Haggai the prophet and Zechariah the prophet, a descendant of Iddo, prophesied to the Jews in Judah and Jerusalem in the name of the God of Israel, who was over them.[2] Then Zerubbabel son of Shealtiel and Joshua son of Jozadak set to work to rebuild the house of God in Jerusalem. And the prophets of God were with them, supporting them.

[3] At that time Tattenai, governor of Trans-Euphrates, and Shethar-Bozenai and their associates went to them and asked, "Who authorized you to rebuild this temple and to finish it?" [4] They also asked, "What are the names of those who are constructing this building?" [5] But the eye of their God was watching over the elders of the Jews, and they were not stopped until a report could go to Darius and his written reply be received.

[6] This is a copy of the letter that Tattenai, governor of Trans-Euphrates, and Shethar-Bozenai and their associates, the officials of Trans-Euphrates, sent to King Darius. [7] The report they sent him read as follows:

To King Darius:

Cordial greetings.

[8] The king should know that we went to the district of Judah, to the temple of the great God. The people are building it with large stones and placing the timbers in the walls. The work is being carried on with diligence and is making rapid progress under their direction.

[9] We questioned the elders and asked them, "Who authorized you to rebuild this temple and to finish it?" [10] We also asked them their names, so that we could write down the names of their leaders for your information.

[11] This is the answer they gave us:

"We are the servants of the God of heaven and earth, and we are rebuilding the temple that was built many years ago, one that a great king of Israel built and finished. [12] But because our ancestors angered the God of heaven, he gave them into the hands of Nebuchadnezzar the Chaldean, king of Babylon, who destroyed this temple and deported the people to Babylon.

[13] "However, in the first year of Cyrus king of Babylon, King Cyrus issued a decree to rebuild this house of God. [14] He even removed from the temple of Babylon the gold and silver articles of the house of God, which Nebuchadnezzar had taken from the temple in Jerusalem and brought to the temple in

121

Babylon. Then King Cyrus gave them to a man named Sheshbazzar, whom he had appointed governor, [15] and he told him, 'Take these articles and go and deposit them in the temple in Jerusalem. And rebuild the house of God on its site.'

[16] "So this Sheshbazzar came and laid the foundations of the house of God in Jerusalem. From that day to the present it has been under construction but is not yet finished."

[17] Now if it pleases the king, let a search be made in the royal archives of Babylon to see if King Cyrus did in fact issue a decree to rebuild this house of God in Jerusalem. Then let the king send us his decision in this matter.

Ezra 6   The Decree of Darius

[1] King Darius then issued an order, and they searched in the archives stored in the treasury at Babylon. [2] A scroll was found in the citadel of Ecbatana in the province of Media, and this was written on it:

Memorandum:

[3] In the first year of King Cyrus, the king issued a decree concerning the temple of God in Jerusalem:

Let the temple be rebuilt as a place to present sacrifices, and let its foundations be laid. It is to be sixty cubits high and sixty cubits wide, [4] with three courses of large stones and one of timbers. The costs are to be paid by the royal treasury. [5] Also, the gold and silver articles of the house of God, which Nebuchadnezzar took from the temple in Jerusalem and brought to Babylon, are to be returned to their places in the temple in Jerusalem; they are to be deposited in the house of God.

[6] Now then, Tattenai, governor of Trans-Euphrates, and Shethar-Bozenai and you other officials of that province, stay away from there. [7] Do not interfere with the work on this temple of God. Let the governor of the Jews and the Jewish elders rebuild this house of God on its site. [8] Moreover, I hereby decree what you are to do for these elders of the Jews in the construction of this house of God: Their expenses are to be fully paid out of the royal treasury, from the revenues of Trans-Euphrates, so that the work will not stop.

[9] Whatever is needed—young bulls, rams, male lambs for burnt offerings to the God of heaven, and wheat, salt, wine and olive oil, as requested by the priests in Jerusalem—must be given them daily without fail, [10] so that they may offer sacrifices pleasing to the God of heaven and pray for the well-being of the king and his sons.

[11] Furthermore, I decree that if anyone defies this edict, a beam is to be pulled from their house and they are to be impaled on it. And for this crime their house is to be made a pile of rubble. [12] May God, who has caused his Name to dwell there, overthrow any king or people who lifts a hand to change this decree or to destroy this temple in Jerusalem.

I Darius have decreed it. Let it be carried out with diligence.

Completion and Dedication of the Temple

[13] Then, because of the decree King Darius had sent, Tattenai, governor of Trans-Euphrates, and Shethar-Bozenai and their associates carried it out with diligence. [14] So the elders of the Jews continued to build and prosper under the preaching of Haggai the prophet and Zechariah, a descendant of Iddo. They finished building the temple according to the command of the God of Israel and the decrees of Cyrus, Darius and Artaxerxes, kings of Persia. [15] The temple was completed on the third day of the month Adar, in the sixth year of the reign of King Darius.

[16] Then the people of Israel—the priests, the Levites and the rest of the exiles—celebrated the dedication of the house of God with joy. [17] For the dedication of this house of God they offered a hundred bulls, two hundred rams, four hundred male lambs and, as a sin offering for all Israel, twelve male goats, one for each of the tribes of Israel. [18] And they installed the priests in their divisions and the Levites in their groups for the service of God at Jerusalem, according to what is written in the Book of Moses.

The Passover

[19] On the fourteenth day of the first month, the exiles celebrated the Passover. [20] The priests and Levites had purified themselves and were all ceremonially clean. The Levites slaughtered the Passover lamb for all the exiles, for their relatives the priests and for themselves. [21] So the Israelites who had returned from the exile ate it, together with all who had separated themselves from the unclean practices of their Gentile neighbors in order to seek the LORD, the God of Israel. [22] For seven days they celebrated with joy the Festival of Unleavened Bread, because the LORD had filled them with joy by changing the attitude of the king of Assyria so that he assisted them in the work on the house of God, the God of Israel.

Psalms of the Exiles
Psalms 74, 85, 126, 138, and 139:1-12

Psalm 74

A maskil of Asaph.

1 O God, why have you rejected us forever?
    Why does your anger smolder against the sheep of your pasture?
2 Remember the nation you purchased long ago,
    the people of your inheritance, whom you redeemed—
    Mount Zion, where you dwelt.
3 Turn your steps toward these everlasting ruins,
    all this destruction the enemy has brought on the sanctuary.
4 Your foes roared in the place where you met with us;
    they set up their standards as signs.
5 They behaved like men wielding axes
    to cut through a thicket of trees.
6 They smashed all the carved paneling
    with their axes and hatchets.
7 They burned your sanctuary to the ground;
    they defiled the dwelling place of your Name.
8 They said in their hearts, "We will crush them completely!"
    They burned every place where God was worshiped in the land.
9 We are given no signs from God;
    no prophets are left,
    and none of us knows how long this will be.
10 How long will the enemy mock you, God?
    Will the foe revile your name forever?
11 Why do you hold back your hand, your right hand?
    Take it from the folds of your garment and destroy them!
12 But God is my King from long ago;
    he brings salvation on the earth.
13 It was you who split open the sea by your power;
    you broke the heads of the monster in the waters.
14 It was you who crushed the heads of Leviathan
    and gave it as food to the creatures of the desert.
15 It was you who opened up springs and streams;
    you dried up the ever-flowing rivers.
16 The day is yours, and yours also the night;
    you established the sun and moon.
17 It was you who set all the boundaries of the earth;
    you made both summer and winter.
18 Remember how the enemy has mocked you, LORD,
    how foolish people have reviled your name.
19 Do not hand over the life of your dove to wild beasts;
    do not forget the lives of your afflicted people forever.

²⁰ Have regard for your covenant,
   because haunts of violence fill the dark places of the land.
²¹ Do not let the oppressed retreat in disgrace;
   may the poor and needy praise your name.
²² Rise up, O God, and defend your cause;
   remember how fools mock you all day long.
²³ Do not ignore the clamor of your adversaries,
   the uproar of your enemies, which rises continually.

Psalm 85

For the director of music. Of the Sons of Korah. A psalm.
¹ You, LORD, showed favor to your land;
   you restored the fortunes of Jacob.
² You forgave the iniquity of your people
   and covered all their sins.
³ You set aside all your wrath
   and turned from your fierce anger.
⁴ Restore us again, God our Savior,
   and put away your displeasure toward us.
⁵ Will you be angry with us forever?
   Will you prolong your anger through all generations?
⁶ Will you not revive us again,
   that your people may rejoice in you?
⁷ Show us your unfailing love, LORD,
   and grant us your salvation.
⁸ I will listen to what God the LORD says;
   he promises peace to his people, his faithful servants—
   but let them not turn to folly.
⁹ Surely his salvation is near those who fear him,
   that his glory may dwell in our land.
¹⁰ Love and faithfulness meet together;
   righteousness and peace kiss each other.
¹¹ Faithfulness springs forth from the earth,
   and righteousness looks down from heaven.
¹² The Lord will indeed give what is good,
   and our land will yield its harvest.
¹³ Righteousness goes before him
   and prepares the way for his steps.

Psalm 126

A song of ascents.

[1] When the LORD restored the fortunes of Zion,
  we were like those who dreamed.
[2] Our mouths were filled with laughter,
  our tongues with songs of joy.
Then it was said among the nations,
  "The LORD has done great things for them."
[3] The LORD has done great things for us,
  and we are filled with joy.
[4] Restore our fortunes, LORD,
  like streams in the Negev.
[5] Those who sow with tears
  will reap with songs of joy.
[6] Those who go out weeping,
  carrying seed to sow,
will return with songs of joy,
  carrying sheaves with them.

Psalm 138

Of David.

[1] I will praise you, LORD, with all my heart;
  before the "gods" I will sing your praise.
[2] I will bow down toward your holy temple
  and will praise your name
  for your unfailing love and your faithfulness,
for you have so exalted your solemn decree
  that it surpasses your fame.
[3] When I called, you answered me;
  you greatly emboldened me.
[4] May all the kings of the earth praise you, LORD,
  when they hear what you have decreed.
[5] May they sing of the ways of the LORD,
  for the glory of the LORD is great.
[6] Though the LORD is exalted, he looks kindly on the lowly;
  though lofty, he sees them from afar.
[7] Though I walk in the midst of trouble,
  you preserve my life.
You stretch out your hand against the anger of my foes;
  with your right hand you save me.
[8] The LORD will vindicate me;
  your love, LORD, endures forever—
  do not abandon the works of your hands.

Psalm 139:1-12

For the director of music. Of David. A psalm.
[1] You have searched me, LORD,
   and you know me.
[2] You know when I sit and when I rise;
   you perceive my thoughts from afar.
[3] You discern my going out and my lying down;
   you are familiar with all my ways.
[4] Before a word is on my tongue
   you, LORD, know it completely.
[5] You hem me in behind and before,
   and you lay your hand upon me.
[6] Such knowledge is too wonderful for me,
   too lofty for me to attain.
[7] Where can I go from your Spirit?
   Where can I flee from your presence?
[8] If I go up to the heavens, you are there;
   if I make my bed in the depths, you are there.
[9] If I rise on the wings of the dawn,
   if I settle on the far side of the sea,
[10] even there your hand will guide me,
   your right hand will hold me fast.
[11] If I say, "Surely the darkness will hide me
   and the light become night around me,"
[12] even the darkness will not be dark to you;
   the night will shine like the day,
   for darkness is as light to you.

Full Notes of God's Rooting Review in Haggai and Zechariah 1
(Based on the Rooted Review's key words as they develop in each of passage)
By Jan C. Thompson

1. GOD KNOWS—Jehovah Sammah The Lord is There (Ezekiel 48:35)
Haggai 1:2 *"This is what the LORD Almighty says: "These people say, 'The time has not yet come to rebuild the LORD's house."*
➤   **God Knows-** what we are thinking and saying.
Haggai 2:2 *"Speak to Zerubbabel son of Shealtiel, governor of Judah, to Joshua son of Jozadak, the high priest, and to the remnant of the people."*
➤   **God Knows-** each one by name--Zerubbabel, Joshua, and remnant.
Zechariah 1:1 *"In the eighth month of the second year of Darius, the word of the Lord came to the prophet Zechariah son of Berekiah, the son of Iddo."*

➤   **God Knows-** our families, world leaders, dates, etc.

Haggai 2:10 *"On the twenty-fourth day of the ninth month, in the second year of Darius, the word of the LORD came to the prophet Haggai:"*

➤   **God Knows-** world leaders, dates, the past and the future of it all.

2. GOD QUESTIONS—Elohim Judge, Creator (Eccl. 3:17, Psalm 50:6)
As the perfect teacher or life coach, He seeks to direct us onto the right path. At the heart of life coaching is creative, thought-provoking questions that seek to direct a person's thinking to pursue new ideas and alternative solutions with greater resiliency in the face of complexity.
Haggai 1:3-4 *"Then the word of the LORD came through the prophet Haggai: 4 "Is it a time for you yourselves to be living in your paneled houses, while this house (My temple) remains a ruin?"*
➤   **God Questions-** He will ask us questions to help us understand detours/mistakes on our journey.
Haggai 2:3 *"Ask them, "Who of you is left who saw this house in its former glory? How does it look to you now? Does it not seem to you like nothing?"*
➤   **God Questions-** He seeks to help us see what is at the root of the problem. He wanted to reveal the goal of building the temple was being undermined by a spirit of complaining and focusing on the wrong vision. Solomon's temple and not the one God wanted them to build after the exile.
Zechariah 1:5-6 *"Where are your ancestors now? And the prophets, do they live forever. 6 But did not my words and my decrees, which I commanded my servants the prophets, overtake your ancestors?"*

➤   **God Questions-** God's questions are to bring perspective to us to learn from the past and not make the same mistakes.

Haggai 2:10-14 *"On the twenty-fourth day of the ninth month, in the second year of Darius, the word of the LORD came to the prophet Haggai: 11 "This is what the LORD Almighty says: 'Ask the priests what the law says:*
12 If someone carries consecrated meat in the fold of their garment, and that fold touches some bread or stew, some wine, olive oil or other food, does it become consecrated?' "
The priests answered, "No."
13 Then Haggai said, "If a person defiled by contact with a dead body touches one of these things, does it become defiled?" "Yes," the priests replied, "it becomes defiled."
14 Then Haggai said, "'So it is with this people and this nation in my sight,' declares the LORD. 'Whatever they do and whatever they offer there is defiled."

➢ **God Questions-** What makes you holy? God speaks to the issue of the heart. Even though they are working hard on the temple, the temple itself will not make them holy. Only God can make us holy.

3.   GOD   CHALLENGES—Jehovah-Tsidkenu   Jehovah-Righteous (Jeremiah 24:5-6)
Haggai 1:5-7 *"Now this is what the LORD Almighty says:"Give careful thought to your ways.*
6 You have planted much, but harvested little. You eat, but never have enough. You drink, but never have your fill. You put on clothes, but are not warm. You earn wages, only to put them in a purse with holes in it."
7 This is what the LORD Almighty says: "Give careful thought to your ways."
➢ **God Challenges-** "Give careful thought to your ways." The challenge is to review our journey and make needed corrections. God's intent was for the people to take time to refect and understand the need for change in their personal life and as a nation.
Haggai 2:4-5 *"But now be strong, Zerubbabel,' declares the LORD. 'Be strong, Joshua son of Jozadak, the high priest. Be strong, all you people of the land,' declares the LORD, 'and work. For I am with you,' declares the LORD Almighty.*
5 'This is what I covenanted with you when you came out of Egypt. And my Spirit remains among you. Do not fear.'"
➢ **God Challenges-** "Be strong!" Do not fear! God called them to begin rebuilding the temple, to focus with all their strength and get it done. Don't be discouraged by those outside or inside your camp that move you to fear. Keep your eyes on Me.
Zechariah 1:2-3 *"The Lord was very angry with your ancestors. 3 Therefore tell the people: This is what the Lord Almighty says; 'Return to me,' declares the Lord Almighty, 'and I will return to you,' says the Lord Almighty."*

➢ **God's Challenges**-f you don't want Me to continue to be angry, "Return to Me" "and I will return to you!" God is ready if we will obey.

Haggai 2:15-16 *"'Now give careful thought to this from this day on—consider how things were before one stone was laid on another in the LORD's temple. 16 When anyone came to a heap of twenty measures, there were only ten. When anyone went to a wine vat to draw fifty measures, there were only twenty."*
➢ **God Challenges-** "Give careful thought to this from this day on— consider how things were before." I will forgive the past "from this day on." Though they had turned to the Lord in the 8th month they need to review their situation from His perspective again if they were going to move forward with His blessing.

4. GOD DIRECTS—Jehovah-Raah Caring Shepherd (Psalm 23:1, Psalm 80:1)
Haggai 1:8-11 *"Go up into the mountains and bring down timber and build my house, so that I may take pleasure in it and be honored," says the LORD. 9 "You expected much, but see, it turned out to be little. What you brought home, I blew away. Why?" declares the LORD Almighty. "Because of my house, which remains a ruin, while each of you is busy with your own house. 10 Therefore, because of you the heavens have withheld their dew and the earth its crops. 11 I called for a drought on the fields and the mountains, on the grain, the new wine, the olive oil and everything else the ground produces, on people and livestock, and on all the labor of your hands."*
➢ **God Directs-** with clear steps of obedience and a reminder that it is not time to disobey by being discouraged any more.
Haggai 2:6-9 *"This is what the LORD Almighty says: 'In a little while I will once more shake the heavens and the earth, the sea and the dry land. 7 I will shake all nations, and what is desired by all nations will come, and I will fill this house with glory,' says the LORD Almighty. 8 'The silver is mine and the gold is mine,' declares the LORD Almighty. 9 'The glory of this present house will be greater than the glory of the former house,' says the LORD Almighty. 'And in this place I will grant peace,' declares the LORD Almighty."*
➢ **God Directs-** God directs their thoughts to His thoughts and the reality of the situation. Isaiah 55:8 "For my thoughts are not your thoughts, neither your ways my ways." I will control the nations and fill this temple with glory in a different way then Solomon's temple-through Jesus entering it 500 years in the future. (Ezekiel 40) If it doesn't seem like there are enough resources, remember I own all the wealth.

Zechariah 1:4 "Do not be like your ancestors, to whom the earlier prophets proclaimed: This is what the Lord Almighty says: 'Turn from your evil ways and your evil practices.' But they would not listen or pay attention to me, declares the Lord."

➤ **God Directs**- "Do not be like your ancestors." "Turn from their evil ways and practices." You do not have to take the same wrong road they took. Listen and pay attention to me and obey.

Haggai 2:17-*19* *"I struck all the work of your hands with blight, mildew and hail, yet you did not return to me,' declares the LORD.*
18 'From this day on, from this twenty-fourth day of the ninth month, give careful thought to the day when the foundation of the LORD's temple was laid. Give careful thought:
19 Is there yet any seed left in the barn? Until now, the vine and the fig tree, the pomegranate and the olive tree have not borne fruit."
➤ **God Directs**- God will continue to bring judgment on our lives if we do not return to Him. He is willing to turn things around from "this day forward", if I'm willing to return to Him in sincere repentance, only then does His blessing come.

5. OUR RESPONSE
Haggai 1:12-15 *"Then Zerubbabel son of Shealtiel, Joshua son of Jozadak, the high priest, and the whole remnant of the people obeyed the voice of the Lord their God and the message of the prophet Haggai, because the Lord their God had sent him. And the people feared the Lord."*
➤ **Our Response**- God challenged them as He does to us today on our journey. Obey the voice of the Lord and the message of His Word.
We need to Understand the Fear of the LORD! (Acrostic developed by Jan C. Thompson)
- **F**orsake
- **E**vil
- **A**cknowledge God in our lives and decisions
- **R**everence Him with our worship and obedience in Haggai 1:13-15

Haggai 2:4b *"'Be strong, all you people of the land,' declares the Lord, 'and work.'"*

➤ **Our Response**- Be strong, don't give into fear on the inside or outside, be focused and do the work God has called us to do.

Zechariah 1:6b *"Then they repented and said, 'The Lord Almighty has done to us what our ways and practices deserve, just as He determined to do.'"*

➤ **Our Response**- Admit our sin and recognize that our sin deserves punishment and that His ways are perfect and determined.

Haggai 2:15, 18 *"Now give careful thought to this from this day on—consider."* (Summary)

➢ **Our Response-** Give careful thought to our ways, be reflective and repentant and return to the Lord.

6. GOD RESOURCES—Jehovah-jireh The Lord will provide (Genesis 22:14)

Haggai 1:13-14 *"Then Haggai, the LORD's messenger, gave this message of the LORD to the people: "I am with you," declares the LORD. 14 So the LORD stirred up the spirit of Zerubbabel son of Shealtiel, governor of Judah, and the spirit of Joshua son of Jozadak, the high priest, and the spirit of the whole remnant of the people. They came and began to work on the house of the LORD Almighty, their God."*
➢ **God Resources-** His continual presence with us. His Spirit's encouragement and empowerment to do what He has called us to do.
Haggai 2:4b-5 *"'For I am with you,' declares the Lord Almighty. 'This is what I covenanted with you when you came out of Egypt. And my Spirit remains among you. Do not fear.'"*
➢ **God Resources-** His faithful and powerful presence. His promises are eternal and will be fulfilled. (Romans 4:21, Psalm 105:8, Psalm 119:116)
Zechariah 1:3b, 6b
2b "'Return to me,' declares the Lord Almighty, 'and I will return to you,' says the Lord Almighty."
6b "'The Lord Almighty has done to us what our ways and practices deserve, just as He determined to do.'"
➢ **God Resources-** His loving and determined way to bring us back to Himself. His unchangeable (immutable) character and righteousness of what He expects of us.
Haggai 2:19b-23 *"'From this day on I will bless you.'" 20 The word of the LORD came to Haggai a second time on the twenty-fourth day of the month: 21 "Tell Zerubbabel governor of Judah that I am going to shake the heavens and the earth. 22 I will overturn royal thrones and shatter the power of the foreign kingdoms. I will overthrow chariots and their drivers; horses and their riders will fall, each by the sword of his brother. 23 "'On that day,' declares the LORD Almighty, 'I will take you, my servant Zerubbabel son of Shealtiel,' declares the LORD, 'and I will make you like my signet ring, for I have chosen you,' declares the LORD Almighty."*

➢ **God Resources-** God's ability and willingness to bless (to bestow good and protection) us. 1. His sovereign plan to overthrow evil. 2. His gracious plan to protect and direct His chosen people.

132

Chart Form of Haggai 1 and 2, and Zechariah 1:1-6

Date—2nd year of King Darius of Persia 520 BC

Haggai 1 (6th month 1st day)   **Haggai 2** (7th month 21st day) and
9th month 24$^{th\ day}$)

(Haggai's 1st Message)   (Haggai's 2nd Message)
GOD'S REVIEW   **GOD'S REVIEW**
1. God Knows (2)   1. God Knows (1-2)

2. God Questions (3-4)

2. God Questions (1-2)

3. God Challenges (4-5)

4. God Directs (6-9)

Zechariah 1st Message (September 8th month)
1:1-6 Summarized in answers below

Haggai (November 9th month 24th day)
2. God Questions (10-14)

3. God Challenges (5-7)   3. God Challenges (15-16)

4. God Directs (8-11)   4. God Directs (17-19)

OUR RESPONSE   **OUR RESPONSE**
1. Obedience (12)   1. Give Careful Thought (15-19)

2. Fear the Lord (12)   2. Return to the Lord (17)
   Forsake Evil
   Acknowledge God in every situation
   Reverence/Worship Him

GOD RESOURCES   **GOD RESOURCES**
1. (13) His Presence   1. (4) (19) His Undeserved Blessing
                                and Presence
                            2. (20-22) His Sovereign Control
2. (14) His Empowerment   3. (23) His Divine Plan for us

Answers to the Chart Form of Haggai 1-2 and Zechariah 1:1-6

Haggai 1:1-14 1st Review (6th month 1st day)
God Knows (2)
He calls us by name
He understands what we are thinking!

God Questions (1-2)
Listen for His questions that speak to our conscience-deeper self/Root of Jesse

God Challenges (5-7)
What are the elements He is highlighting to help me review my journey

God Directs (8-11)
What clear steps of obedience is He putting before us?

Our Response (12)
Obedience
Fear of the Lord:
Forsake
Evil
Acknowledge God in every situation
Reverence/Worship Him)

God Resources
(13) His Presence
(14) His Empowerment

Haggai 2:1-9 2nd Review (August 7th month 21st day)
God Knows (1-2)
 Zerubbabel
 Joshua
 Remnant

God Questions (3-4)
 Who of you is left who saw former glory—older people
 How does it look to you now?
 Does it seem like nothing?

God Directs Us (6-9)
 Be strong
 Work
 Do not Fear

Zechariah 1:1-6 3rd Review (September 8th month)

God Knows (1-2)

His present and past people. He will use them as examples and warnings.

God Questions - Note the questions come at the end of his message

God Challenges (3)

If you don't want me to get angry, "Return to Me" and
"I will return to you!

The Lord directs but couples His directive of what He will do
    to shepherd His people.

God Directs (4)

Don't be like your ancestors, to whom the earlier prophets told them to
"Turn from their evil way."

Listen and pay attention to Me.

God Questions (5)

Where are your ancestors now?
    And the prophets, do they live forever?
    But did not my words and my decrees, which I commanded my
    servants the prophets, overtake your ancestors?

Our Response (6)

Admit our sin.

Recognize that our sin deserves punishment, or the redirection God
sees is best. Recognize that His ways are eternally perfect and
determined. Learn from the journeys of the people before us.

God Resources (2)

"Declares the Lord Almighty, 'and I will return to you,' says the
Lord Almighty."

Haggai 2:1-23 4th Review (November 9th month 24th day)

God Questions (10-14)

Does a consecrated thing make other things holy? NO
Does a defiled thing make other things defiled? YES

God Challenges (15-16)

Consider the past
Consider this day forward

God Directs (17-19)

Return to me from this day forward

Our Response	God Resources
Giver Careful Thought (15-19)	(4) (9) God's Undeserved Blessing and Presence
Return to the Lord (17)	(20-22) God's Sovereign Control

UpRooted By God's Design Book Song Playlist
All songs by Tiffany Thompson

Locations to link to the playlist and listen to Tiffany's songs:
Jan Thompson's website: jancthompson.com or
Jan's Link Tree account: https://linktr.ee/jancthompson
for quick access to the playlist on Spotify, iTunes, Amazon Music,
and SoundCloud music-streaming services.

Contents of song lyrics in the book

Introduction Weeks 1-3	
Guideposts for Our UpRooted Journey	11
Week 1 Guideposts from Our Past UpRooted Journey	13
Day 2 Song "Smoke and Fire"	17
Day 4 Song "Past This End"	21
Day 5 Song "New Communions"	23
Week 2 Guideposts for Our Present UpRooted Journey	27
Day 6 Song "Bed of Decision"	29
Day 8 Song "In the Distance"	33
Day 10 Song "Home"	37
Week 3 Guideposts for Our Future UpRooted Journey	41
Day 13 Song "We Are the Dreamers"	47
Day 14 Song "Real Joy"	49
Day 15 Song "Love's Set Aside"	52
Introduction Weeks 4-6	57
God's Rooted Review for Our UpRooted Journey	
Week 4 God's 1st Rooting Review—God's Time	59
Day 17 Song "One Voice"	63
Day 18 Song "Let It Break Through"	65
Day 19 Song "Take It and Run"	67
Day 20 Song "Band Together"	70
Week 5 God's 2nd Rooting Review—God's Plan	73
God's 3rd Rooting Review—God's Call	78
God's 4th Rooting Review—God's Word (Part 1)	
Day 25 Song "Dirty Wings"	84
Week 6 God's 4th Rooting Review—God's Word (Part 2)	87
God's Rooting Reviews Applied	90
Day 30 Song "Soul of the Nation"	99
Conclusion ReRooting by God's Design	103

Notes
UpRooted by God's Design Resources

Bible Reference and Commentary Books

- Baldwin, Joyce, *Haggai, Zechariah, Malachi* (Chicago, IL: Intervarsity Press, 1972).
- Ironside, H.A., *Notes on the Minor Prophets* (New Jersey: Loizeaux Brothers, Inc., 1906).
- James, Rick, *White Papers, Critical Concepts Series Volume 1: The Art of Discerning God's Will* (Orlando, FL: CRU Press, 2012).
- Jensen, Irving L., *Haggai, Zechariah, & Malachi* (Chicago, IL: Moody, 1976).
- Levy, David M., *When Prophets Speak of Judgment* (Bellmawr, NJ: The Friends of Israel Gospel Ministry, 1998).
- Mears, Dr. Henrietta, *What the Bible is All About: Bible Handbook* (Ventura, CA: Regal Books, 1953).
- Morgan, G. Campbell, D.D., *Searchlights from The Word* (Old Tappan, New Jersey: Revell Company, 1977).
- Parker, Joseph, D.D., *The People's Bible: Discourses Upon Holy Scripture, Vol. X, 2 Chronicles XXI—Esther* (New York, NY: Funk & Wagnalls Company, 1887).
- Perowne, J.J. Stewart, D.D., *The Book of Psalms Vol. 1 & 2* (Grand Rapids, MI: Zondervan, 1966).
- Phillips, John, *Exploring the Scriptures* (Chicago, IL: Moody Press, 1965).
- Stedman, Ray C., *Adventuring Through the Bible* (Grand Rapids, MI: Discovery House Publishers, 1997).
- Stibbs, Alan M., editor, *Search the Scriptures* (England: Inter-Varsity Fellowship, 1971).
- The Navigators Life Change Series, *Minor Prophets 2-Nahum, Habakkuk, Zephaniah, Haggai, Zechariah, & Malachi* (Colorado Springs, CO: NavPress, 2014).
- Thompson, Jan C., *Rooted Woman of Valor* (Chicago, IL: CreateSpace, 2017).
- Thompson, Richard Gentry, *Wild Goose Honks 40 Days of Encouragement for Church Leaders* (Minneapolis, MN: NextSteps Resources, 2020).
- van Dyck, Vanessa and Rhome, *The Gospel in Haggai* (Plano, TX: Sacra Script Ministries, 2011).
- Walvoord, John F., and Zuck, Roy B., *The Bible Knowledge Commentary Old Testament* (Wheaton, IL: Scripture Press/Victor Books, 1985).

Music
- Thompson, Tiffany Danae, singer-songwriter's music is available on her website, tiffanythompsonmusic.com, iTunes, Amazon Music, and Spotify.
- Lake, Brandon, "Fear is Not My Future" on the album with Kirk Franklin, Chandler Moore, "Kingdom Book One", (Released 2022).

Pamphlets
- *Bible Timeline Genesis to Revelation—2200 BC—AD100* (Torrance, CA: Rose Publishers, 2001).
- *Chronology of the Bible* (Torrance, CA: Rose Publishers, 2020).
- *The Feasts of the Bible* (Torrance, CA: Rose Publishers, 2011).
- *The Tabernacle* (Torrance, CA: Rose Publishers, 2006).
- *The Temple* (Torrance, CA: Rose Publishers, 2005).

Online Resources
- Raystedman.org, a great resource of inductive, expository messages from Old and New Testaments by Ray Stedman.
- SacraScript.org, Bible timeline resource-and their online app.

Daily Devotional Pattern Books
- Bennett, Arthur, editor, *The Valley of Vision* (Carlisle, PA: The Banner of Truth Trust, 1997).
- Boa, Kenneth, *Face to Face* (Grand Rapids, MI: Zondervan, 1997).
- Elliot, Elizabeth, *A Heart for God: 31 Days to Discover God's Love for You* (Siloam Springs, AR: DaySpring, 2022).
- Foster, Richard J., and Smith, James Bryan, *Devotional Classics* (San Francisco, CA: Harper Collins Publishers, 1993).
- Foster, Richard J., and Griffin, Emilie, *Spiritual Classics* (San Francisco, CA: Harper Collins Publishers, 2000).
- Job, Ruben P. and Shawchuck, Norman, *A Guide to Prayer for Ministers and Other Servants* (Nashville, TN: The Upper Room, 1983).
- Job, Rueben P., *Spiritual Life in the Congregation Retreat* (Nashville, TN: The Upper Room, 1986).
- Keller, W. Phillip, *As a Tree Grows* (Grand Rapids, MI: Fleming H Revell, 1966).
- Leaf, Dr. Caroline, *Switch on Your Brain* (Grand Rapids, MI: Baker Books, 2017).
- Leaf, Dr. Caroline, *Think, Learn, and Succeed: Understanding and Using Your Mind to Thrive at School, the Workplace, and Life* (Grand Rapids, MI: Baker Books, 2018).

- Mother Teresa, *Loving Jesus* (Ann Arbor, MI: Servant Publications, 1991).
- Shawchuck, Norman, and Job Rueben P., *How to Conduct Spiritual Life Retreat* (Nashville, TN: The Upper Room, 1986).
- Thomas, Gary, *Sacred Pathways* (Grand Rapids, MI: Zondervan, 1996).
- Various authors, *Footprints for Pilgrims* (Bombay, India: Gospel Literature Service, 1970).
- Willard, Dallas, *Spirit of Disciplines* (New York: HarperCollins, 1998).
- Zimmerman, Martha, *Celebrate the Feasts* (Minneapolis, MN: Bethany House Publishers, 1981).

Contact Information

UpRooted by God's Design
30 Day Spiritual Journey Devotional
Rooted in Ezra 1-6, Haggai, and Zechariah 1
by Jan C. Thompson
can be purchased on Amazon.com.

UpRooted by God's Design **Book Song Playlist**
Available on:
Jan Thompson's Website: jancthompson.com
(The book song playlist is easy to access on the main page.)
Or on:
Jan's Link Tree account: https://linktr.ee/jancthompson
for quick access to the playlist on Spotify, iTunes, Amazon Music,
and SoundCloud music-streaming services.

Jan C. Thompson's 1st book:
Rooted Woman of Valor
Rooted in Proverbs 31
is also available on Amazon.com for purchase.

Note: The books and music are available for
presentation in message, retreat, and concert format.

For more information contact:

Jan C. Thompson
Email: jancthompson@gmail.com
Website: jancthompson.com

Tiffany Thompson
Email: tiffanyt@tiffanythompsonmusic.com
Website: tiffanythompsonmusic.com
Tiffany Thompson Music is available on Spotify, iTunes,
Amazon Music, and other music-streaming services.

Made in United States
Troutdale, OR
11/15/2023

14606682R00080